TESTIMONIES
OF
GOD'S LOVE

BOOK 4

Cover Design by bespokebookcovers.com

ISBN: 978-0-9962166-9-2

TESTIMONIES

OF

GOD'S LOVE

BOOK 4

Del Hall and Del Hall IV

Acknowledgments

It is with the deepest love and gratitude we thank all those who contributed to this book. The willingness to share some of their sacred experiences made this book possible. These testimonies show that so much more is possible in your relationship with God. We hope that reading them will inspire you to more fully accept the Hand of God.

The authors would also like to thank all those who helped in the editing of this book: Joan Clickner, Lorraine Fortier, and Terry Kisner. Your keen eyes and thoughtful suggestions made a huge difference in the telling of these profound stories.

"The days of any religion or path coming between me and my children are coming to an end" saith the Lord

December 29, 2013

Table of Contents

~~~~~~~~~~~~~~~~~~~~~~~~

Appendix

Foreword

About twenty-five years ago, when my wife Diane and I had two young children, I contracted a life-threatening blood infection. Our family doctor sent us directly to the hospital so I could receive antibiotics intravenously. I was admitted into a room, hooked up to an IV unit, and then watched as Diane took Sam and Michelle home for the night. As they walked away down the long hospital hallway my heart sank, because I realized how serious the situation was. The precious future with my young family was unexpectedly at risk. I then had a very direct conversation with the doctor. He gave me a fifty-fifty chance of survival, depending on whether or not the infection reached my heart that night.

I lay awake much of the night checking the progression of my swollen lymph nodes. What had started on the back of my head had made its way down my neck to my left armpit as it neared my heart. I admit I had never been much for prayer to that point in life, but in that moment of crisis I turned to God. When I did so I soon became calm and peaceful, even though that could have been my last night in this lifetime. The peace came from a growing certainty that God was right there with me and that my life was safely in His Hands. God made this clear to me. In my time of great need God's loving Presence filled my heart, pushing out fear and worry. My biggest concern was for my wife and children. I asked God if I could please survive to help Diane raise Sam and Michelle. At that moment I knew even more deeply that God loved me, was right there with me, and was listening to my heart's prayer. I was comforted by God's closeness. I soon began to feel better and stronger. I knew in my heart I would live even before the doctor confirmed it the next morning. I fell into a sound, healing sleep for the rest of the night. God blessed me with a miracle healing.

Since that critical night in the hospital I have lived a life full of God's blessings. Diane and I have shared the joys of raising our children. We have cherished many pets that opened our hearts. God has blessed us with wonderful friends and good health. We look forward to grandchildren someday. In these ways my spoken prayer that night has been answered many times over. God has blessed me beyond what I could have imagined for myself.

God also heard other prayers in my heart. These prayers were buried so deeply that I did not yet know they existed. God led me to His true Prophet, and he is the key to these deeply buried prayers in my heart. Since then Prophet Del Hall III has helped uncover these deeper prayers. I have a prayer to know God closely and feel His Love deeply. Prophet is teaching me to look differently at life so I can more clearly see that my life is literally in God's loving Hands, an answer to my prayer. Prophet has also lifted me into the Heavens where I have been immersed in God's Love many times. I had another prayer which was to tell God that I love Him. Prophet answered this prayer by teaching me to sing HU, a love song to God. The Prophet has also lifted me, as Soul, into the Heavens so that I can directly tell God that I love him. He is my lifeline to God and he is the way to God. God's chosen Prophet is the distributor of God's Love and blessings to me and all Souls.

I experienced God's loving Presence that critical night in the hospital. His Presence brought me peace and comfort. God heard and answered my spoken prayer to survive. He not only gave me the longer life I asked for, but made it an abundant life full of love, joy, peace, security, knowingness, and countless other blessings. Prophet has taught me that God is always with me, not just when I am calling out to Him in a time of dire need. He has shown me that God hears all my prayers and knows which, when, and how to answer them. That night in the hospital was the first time I knowingly experienced God's loving Presence and felt such peace and comfort in an extreme circumstance. Through the teachings of Prophet and singing HU every day, I am increasingly aware of God's blessings that sweeten every aspect of my life. God has blessed me greatly in so many ways as He blesses all His children. I am very grateful to be aware of these gifts of love!

God's blessings come in endless form and variety. They are personally tailored for each of us, His children. I hope that the authors' testimonies in this book will open up new ways for you to see God's blessings in your own life.

Written by Irv Kempf

Student at Guidance for a Better Life since 1994

Introduction

Welcome to book four of our "Testimonies of God's Love" series. Within these pages are fifty true stories that show the Hand of God reaching out to His children. This book, like our other books, celebrates the many varied ways God expresses His Love. God demonstrates His Love every day, but it often goes unrecognized. It is our hope that by reading these heart-warming testimonies you will learn to more fully recognize and accept God's Love in your own life. God's Love manifests in many ways from the dramatic to the very subtle. When you consciously recognize that God loves you, it can change your life. These authors have experienced this firsthand and are now building their lives on a solid foundation of knowing God personally loves them. They wish to pay it forward by helping you to do the same. Even if you recognize Divine love in your life, it is a profound blessing for God to remind you daily of His Love for you.

One of the first spiritual truths to consider, so you may more fully understand and enjoy this book, is that you do not "have" a Soul. The truth is, you ARE Soul. You are an eternal spiritual being within a temporal physical embodiment, which is to say you are Soul that has a body. In some of these stories the authors spiritually traveled into the Heavens. They traveled not in their physical bodies but as Soul. This is much like when Saint Paul shared that he knew someone who was caught up to the third Heaven. Soul can travel free of the body while still living. When the body does come to its end, the real you, SOUL, will continue on. Once again, you do not *have* a Soul; you *are* Soul that *has* a body. This seemingly simple change in perspective is actually of monumental significance. It is one of the core spiritual truths taught and experienced at Guidance for a Better Life and reflected within the testimonies of this book. When considered, or ideally experienced for yourself, it can open doors to even greater heights of wisdom, love, and understanding.

What then is Soul? In essence, Soul is an individualized piece of the Holy Spirit. We are not God, nor will we ever become God, but in a very real sense Soul is a piece of the Voice of God, the Holy Spirit. This is the true meaning behind the statement of being created in the image of God. Soul is a piece of the Holy Spirit, individualized and personalized through lifetimes of experience.

Life is busy and full of distractions making it easy to forget we are children of God, not just physical bodies. This is one reason why God always sends mankind His ordained Prophet. We need someone who sees clearly, can gently remind us that we are Soul, and who can help us soar free as spiritual eagles. God's Prophet can teach us the "Language of the Divine," the true native tongue of Soul. Then we may recognize and understand the Divine guidance that is always available for us! Fortunately, mankind is never without a Prophet. We are never alone. This is the greatest proof of God's Love for man — a continuous unbroken chain of divinely chosen and trained Prophets sent to help show us our way home to the Heart of God. As the current Prophet my father, Del Hall III, is now in this role and has been authorized to share God's Light, Love, and truth with the world.

This book is ultimately a celebration of God's Love for Soul and the many ways He expresses His Love. It is not an attempt to place a wedge between you and another spiritual teacher; it is intended to enhance whatever spiritual path you may be on, even if that is no path at all. As you may read in the Appendix, "What is the Role of God's Prophet?" you do not have to withdraw your love from a former Prophet (one who is no longer here in the physical) to benefit from being taught by the current Prophet. Having a guide who can teach you the Ways and Truths of God in both the inner spiritual worlds and also in the physical is such a blessing. Even so, if you are not comfortable accepting help from the current Prophet, there are still blessings within these pages for you. If you read this book with an open heart the testimonies within have the potential of greatly blessing you.

It is with great humility, reverence, and love that these authors share their experiences, blessings, and insights with you. They know God is truly reaching out through His Prophet to develop a more personal and loving relationship with each and every one of us. They know you too can experience even greater joy and abundance in your life by opening yourself to the truth within these pages — a truth that has the power to set you free and provide guidance for a better life.

Del Hall IV

Note to the Reader

All the authors who contributed to this book sing HU daily in spiritual contemplation. They tune in and raise up spiritually by singing HU, which makes them more receptive to the guidance and Love of God and God's Prophet. A basic understanding of both the role of God's Prophet and HU will help you more fully understand the "Language of the Divine" shared in this book. Please refer to the Appendix for an introductory understanding of God's historical line of Prophets and the role they serve.

HU is an ancient name for God that can be sung quietly or aloud in prayer. HU has existed since the beginning of time in one form or another and is available to all regardless of religion. It is a pure way to express your love to God and give thanks for your blessings.

Singing HU (HUUUUUU, pronounced "hue") serves as a tuning fork with Spirit that brings you into greater harmony with the Divine. We recommend singing HU a few minutes each day. This can bring love, joy, peace, and clarity, or help you rise to a higher view of a situation when upset or fearful.

1

Serious Car Accident Avoided

God can communicate with each of His children. This communication comes in many ways and sometimes is so subtle we could easily disregard it. Learning to recognize, trust, and act on this guidance can save not only our lives, but the lives of those around us.

Occasionally I have to travel for work. One Saturday in December I had an out-of-state job in Maryland, about a three and a half hour drive from my home. The weather report indicated there was a seventy percent chance of snow in the morning. I set my alarm for 5:45 am. Something woke me up several minutes before the alarm went off so I got ready and headed out a little earlier than expected. A beautiful light snow was falling as I drove out of my neighborhood and into the mountains.

I enjoy singing HU throughout my day and have been doing so for years. I put a HU CD on in my car to listen to as I left my house. The HU is a beautiful love song to God. It helps me relax, be in the moment, fills me with peace, love, joy, and helps me walk through my day more gracefully. Today it also brought protection. While singing HU that morning, I was very aware of my spiritual teacher's presence with me on the inner. I have grown to realize this relationship is the key to everything good in my life.

Snow was starting to stick to the mountain roads and they were becoming a little slippery. I prayed to God for a safe drive. Shortly after I crossed the mountain the temperature rose above freezing causing the snow to change to rain. Though it rained the entire time, I drove for the next two hours up to the Washington DC area without incident.

The speed of the traffic around the DC beltway was about fifty-five to sixty miles per hour. Everything was going smoothly when "out of the blue" I got a brief thought or image of a car on the highway spinning out of control. Though it seemed to be a random or unusual thought, from years of experience I trusted and knew I should pay attention. I took my foot off the gas and stepped on the brake to slow down. The vehicles behind me also slowed down.

Shortly after I decreased my speed a lady in a green Jeep Cherokee, two vehicles ahead of mine, lost control of her car. She swerved across three lanes of traffic and smashed into the concrete highway divider. Her car bounced and spun out of control back across the highway. The man to the left of me locked up his brakes and fishtailed toward her. He just missed hitting her by inches. Eventually her car stopped sideways in the middle of the road. Had I not slowed down I would have hit her broadside. We were on a curve in the road and many cars behind us were still approaching. Some of the drivers had probably seen the brake lights or what had just happened and slowed down, though there were others coming around the bend who were caught off guard. I had a strong feeling to keep moving because this was not a safe place to be. I drove past the lady in the car and saw her airbag had deployed. She looked like she was shaken but seemed okay. I pulled over past the accident and out of danger and called 911.

Through this experience I know God's Love and Grace had once again blessed my life. The Hand of God and the protection of the HU saved me from a major car accident. I was given a subtle warning. If I had not trusted that inner guidance and immediately followed that nudge to slow down, I could have crashed into her vehicle. If I had not been awakened a few minutes earlier than my alarm was set for, I could have been in this accident, or I could have been stuck behind it for hours and would not have made it to my job on time. Perhaps the biggest gift of God putting me in that particular spot on that particular day was that several of the cars behind me also avoided being in a very serious accident.

Written by Jason Levinson

2

Call Your Trainer — One Hour Window

❧

As convenient as modern technology can be, it has its obvious limits. If you don't have your phone, you're not getting the call. If your internet is down, you're not seeing your emails. Fortunately, the "inner" communication of Soul is always up and running and can get the message through to those who know the "Language of the Divine."

It is amazing and beautiful how God's timing works. Several years ago I did a search on Craigslist for a personal trainer to help me get in physical shape. I said a prayer and asked for God's guidance to know which trainer would be the right one, and God knew. After talking to several people at gyms and fitness facilities, I was led to the right person. We trained in his fiancée's garage — not in a typical gym. This was perfect.

We had fun working out and began talking about God, events from our childhood, and the everyday ups and downs in life. We were getting in shape both physically and spiritually. As we talked we saw the blessings and miracles in our lives. We looked deeper into the events happening to us and appreciated God's guidance. We discussed how going through tough lessons in life has made us stronger, and as we went through them, we knew we were not alone. God has been there every step of the way. The year we spent training brought our families together; I became the sister he never had. We kind of adopted one another. We do not always have time to talk on a regular basis, yet we know we are there for one another.

I had a part-time job between Thanksgiving and Christmas, and I was working double shifts so it did not leave me much free time. One Friday afternoon as I left work I got a strong nudge to call my trainer. It was the end of a very long week and all I wanted to do was get something to eat and go to bed. Instead I scrolled through my phone for his number to call him anyway. As I did so, my thumb hit the wrong contact. Yes, I thought to myself, I would like to talk to that person, but not now. I kept scrolling and again pushed the wrong contact. I still had this strong urge that I had to talk with my trainer. Finally I got the right number.

I called but there was no answer, so I left a message. He called back. I said, "Hey, how are you and the family doing?" He replied, "We are all doing good, I'm a little stressed right now. Are you going to be there?" I asked what he was talking about. "I have been trying to get a hold of you for two weeks now. I dropped my phone in the toilet and lost all my contact numbers. My fiancée and I are getting married in one hour." I was surprised and asked him to repeat what he said. "We are getting married at the township magistrate in one hour. Can you be there?" "Ahhhh, yeah, but I am still in my work clothes and I do not have time to go home and change." He told me it did not matter, that my being there is what mattered to him and his fiancée. He asked, "Did you get my email with the details?" I said, "No, what email? I have not received anything. I am just following the nudge I got to call you." I asked if he had said any prayers and he answered, "Yes, I prayed last night and asked God for someone from my family to be there for me." I said, "Well, your prayers were heard and answered." So, I turned the car around and headed to the marriage ceremony.

As a student at Guidance for a Better Life I have learned to listen to and follow nudges, which are a form of Divine communication. Every time I do, it turns out to be a blessing. I am so grateful God communicates with me in this way. It was beautiful to see my adopted brother and his fiancée get married. Thank you Prophet.

Written by Rebecca Vettorel

3

Blessed to Be a Witness

❧

Being at the hospital offering love and support to a loved one is a blessing. In the following story the author was not able to be there physically but was taken spiritually by Prophet for a visit. The blessings of God's Love she witnessed went way beyond a single hospital room.

Several years ago my heart was heavy. I had recently found out someone I care about very much had cancer. It had been a long and trying time to get to the diagnosis. Once it came, the doctors very quickly recommended surgery as the best course of action.

I wanted to be there for her, but it was not feasible at the time. My thoughts were with her and her immediate family throughout the entire process. I had a desire to help however I could so I made family phone calls, coordinated efforts, and sent care packages, but I felt there was more I could be doing. I knew I could pray, so I did.

A couple of days after her surgery, I attended a retreat at Guidance for a Better Life. Prophet Del Hall led the group in singing HU, a love song to God. As we sang, God's Love rained down in golden drops of light like a shower washing over me, and I felt so much love. I saw my loved ones at the hospital in and around her bed. I stood next to Prophet in the recovery room and noticed it was filled with Divine love that felt comforting and protecting. My heart smiled with gratitude to know his presence was there. My prayers were answered, and I was blessed with the added gift to actually recognize it. Even though I could not be at the hospital physically during that time, I was able to be there spiritually, which brought me comfort and peace. I did not know what lay on the journey ahead, but I know she and her family were not alone during that difficult time.

As the experience continued Prophet said, "Let's go," and turned to exit the room. I followed, and as we walked down the hall I saw beams of light gently flow from him to each open doorway. Prophet was passing along God's Love to each person and family. Love, comfort, healing, peace — whatever was needed was individually provided as different manifestations of God's Love from that light. These are such beautiful gifts of God's Love through His Prophet. I watched in awe, seeing in a way I had not before; blessed to witness this sacred act and grateful that Prophet bestows these gifts from God.

This experience was a gift on so many levels. Whether they know it or not, my loved ones were blessed. God's Love filled that room in whatever form they needed — love, comfort, peace, strength, and more. I was fortunate to see it and was comforted knowing Prophet was with them. My prayer was answered to be with them and express my love. At the same time I was able to witness Prophet distributing God's Love to many Souls at the hospital. What a beautiful sight to behold.

God loves us and sends His Prophet to help us. I am blessed to have his inner guidance and outer teachings. They help me experience such things and learn the "Language of the Divine" to understand the blessings. I am so grateful for that. It has changed my life and is available for you too.

Written by Michelle Hibshman

4

God's Healing Light

Often we are not aware of the things holding us back spiritually. Fortunately God knows, and if we receive the Light of God into our hearts It can gently remove the blocks that keep us from soaring free. God's Light truly has the power to cleanse, purify, and uplift Soul. It is a gift of love from God to experience It.

It is an amazing gift that God knows us far better than we even know ourselves. Sometimes we do not need to ask for a specific blessing from God. If we have trust in God and ask Him for whatever He knows is in our best interest, the results can be far beyond anything we could have even thought to ask for ourselves.

Years ago during a spiritual retreat at Guidance for a Better Life, Prophet Del Hall led us in a spiritual exercise. During this spiritual experience an enormous wave of God's whitish, golden Light showered down on the group. God's precious Light and Love filled my entire being. As it flowed through me, it washed away things that were holding me back from living a more abundant life. This beautiful Light of God contained countless blessings that were custom-tailored to each and every person receiving them. These blessings were a personal gift from God Himself, in His infinite knowing of what we each need, more than we could possibly even know ourselves.

I consciously surrendered to the Divine and I willingly gave up anything that was not beneficial to me. Anything that could be holding me back spiritually in life, I wanted gone. I saw little dark spots here and there being flushed out by God's cleansing Light. They may have been old habit patterns or ways of thinking that no longer served me well. They may have been things like anger, lust, attachment, fear, or ego that was to some degree holding me back spiritually. They could have even been physical ailments. Not needing to know what exactly I was being cleansed of, I trusted God completely to purify me of what was no longer beneficial to me, and to leave what was good.

The roaring wave of God's Light slowly turned into a gentle trickle of golden light attending to various parts of my being. I felt a sense of precision and gentle care as God's Light washed away the negative things, and refilled those spots with His precious golden Light and Love. After this blessing and gift from God, I was left with an incredible feeling of freedom. I also felt a tremendous lightness as the weight of these things holding me back was cleansed and washed away.

Often we hold on tightly to our imperfections. Even though we know they are holding us back, some part of us identifies with them and resists change. These imperfections are not part of the real us, Soul, a Divine child of God. If we trust completely, and give permission to God and His Prophet to help us grow and evolve, we will live a life of greater abundance. There is no limit to the amount of grace and blessings God can bestow upon us.

Over the fifteen years I have been attending spiritual retreats Guidance for a Better Life, these blessings of healing and growth have occurred dozens and dozens of times. The cumulative effect of God's Love and Grace is astounding. I cannot even imagine what my life would be like today if it were not for the loving spiritual guidance of God's Prophet and the precious love God has given me. Thank you!

Written by Sam Kempf

5

Reassurance Just When I Needed It

One of the greatest blessings is when we receive clarity on a major decision we are trying to make. Spirit can use anything in our life to help deliver this clarity to us. It can also give us the courage to follow our heart and act on the guidance we receive.

It was a difficult decision to move on after twenty-two years in a relationship. For quite some time I had been on the fence about my decision and the indecision was wearing me out, along with the relationship itself. I did not have the energy and courage to follow through. The inner and outer guidance I was getting indicated it was time, or past time, to make the decision and move on. That got my attention, but distractions seemed to keep popping up to delay my taking action.

I decided it would be important for me to attend the May weekend spiritual retreat at Guidance for a Better Life. Prophet provided very helpful clarity and input that weekend, thank you! Nearing the Virginia border on my drive back to Asheville, North Carolina, I thought I heard an alarm clock going off. I closed the car windows and the sound stopped. Well, a few minutes later this whole scenario repeated itself. Again, I closed the windows and the sound stopped. I tried to reach around in the car for where my alarm clock might be, but I could not find it. Normally my travel alarm clock would eventually stop beeping and stop for good. I knew it wasn't the alarm clock because the sequence continued most all the way back to Asheville, and it seemed like a sign.

When I crossed over into Tennessee there was a huge sign saying, "Change is coming. Experience history in August." I had strong inner guidance it would be important to begin getting my things in order. When I got home I had some serious talks with my significant other, although I did not yet have the courage to tell him I wanted to leave. I prayed for assistance from Prophet to find my inner strength and courage.

In June I was again at the retreat center and developing inner strength and courage was one of the areas we focused on during the eight-day retreat. Around that time a movie had come out called "We Bought a Zoo," and one of the pearls shared at the retreat was how the main character only needed twenty seconds of courage to take an important action, which he did, and it changed his life. During the last evening of the retreat our area of Virginia experienced a unique storm, a derecho. We stood outside watching the sky as it sounded like a freight train roaring up the side of the mountain, although the trees did not seem to be moving. The sky was spectacular and looked like a July 4th celebration. During this amazing storm I felt strength in the presence of the Prophet and found a depth of inner strength and courage I had not known before. I was finally at peace. I knew what I needed to do as Soul. It felt like the Divine had done most of the heavy lifting to give me the strength and courage to follow my heart, now I had to do my part!

When I returned home to North Carolina I continued to receive a lot of support and guidance on the outer and inner. A friend suggested I write a letter to my significant other to say what I would want to say, without giving it to him. This would help me focus on what I would want to say in person. I found the suggestion very helpful. In my heart I knew this suggestion, that came through my friend, was from the inner Prophet. As Soul I was getting a deep inner call to make this change, and if I did not heed it I felt I would start dying inside. It was important to me to make this change with love, rather than getting into blame and anger.

The following week while I was at work, I saw a U-Haul truck go by with a huge picture of an Indian woman on the side of it. I ran outside and saw the name of Sacajawea written on the side. This was an awake dream to me because I have a close affinity with that name. During the next few days I researched prices for a U-Haul truck rental to move to Virginia. By the end of the week I had the inner knowingness that it was time. Holding the hand of the inner Prophet I took a deep breath and received the first twenty seconds of courage, and then the next, and the next. I had a long talk and interaction with my significant other. I was able to share with him what I really wanted to convey from a place of love. He and I talked and talked, and cried together. That night was really tough, and I slept restlessly.

As I headed to work the next morning I had doubts as to whether I was making the right decision. I started singing HU, a love song to God, and asked for assistance from Prophet. Rounding the corner into the parking lot at work, lo and behold there was a U-Haul truck sitting smack dab in front of my office. And in big letters on the side it said "VIRGINIA." It was the perfect reassurance I needed at that moment! God's timing is always perfect, impeccable. Thank you dear God and Prophet for your reassurance, comfort, love, and guidance. I appreciate and love you.

Written by Jan Reid

6

My Cat Ace

It is a blessing when you recognize a prayer has been answered. Even more comforting is realizing a prayer of the heart, one you never "officially" prayed for, has been answered. Whether voiced out loud or not, God knows what will bring joy and love into our lives.

It was July 2014 and I was getting ready to move out of my parents' house to live on my own for the first time. Throughout my life I have always had several family pets, and I absolutely adored our family's two cats. When I moved out my parents would be keeping the cats, so I knew eventually I wanted to get a cat of my own.

The week before I was going to move I was at Petco with my boyfriend Eric. We were there on a Sunday afternoon and Petco had many kittens available for adoption that day. Eric and I made the "mistake" of playing with one, and I fell in love with the idea of adopting a kitten. Logically, I thought I should not adopt any of these kittens with my upcoming move to another city and starting a new job. I figured that once I moved and got settled in, I would adopt an adult cat to save it from a shelter, since adult cats do not generally get adopted as quickly as kittens do. By that evening I realized in my heart I really wanted a kitten, not an adult cat. I had never had a kitten before as all of our cats were adopted as adults, and I really wanted to experience watching a kitten grow and develop. I told this to Eric and hoped maybe I would happen to find a stray kitten who needed a loving home. I did not realize in telling Eric this that I was vocalizing a prayer in my heart. Twelve hours later God answered my prayer!

The next morning as I was walking into work, I was preoccupied with the tasks I had to do to prepare for my last week at this job. I almost walked right past a tiny, scared kitten cowering next to the exterior of the building. I stopped in my tracks as I realized I had just seen a kitten! I slowly approached the kitten. I got about four feet away from her and extended my arm. The kitten ran off around the building, very frightened. I did not see where she went. By the Grace of God, a woman who worked with me just happened to be sitting in her car that morning and told me she saw a tiny flash of something run into a hole in the side of the building. I looked into the hole and sure enough there was the kitten, part way up a four-inch wide PVC pipe that extended inside the brick wall. Just then another coworker of mine, April, arrived to work. April came to help me with the kitten, but neither of us could quite reach into the pipe to pull her out. April stayed with the kitten while I went in search of something to place the kitten in if we got her out. I ended up driving home and getting a cat carrier and some cat food to try to entice her out of the wall. Eventually, the kitten slipped down enough that April was able to reach her hind legs to pull her out. I held the carrier as April released a very dirty, skinny, tick covered, and frightened kitten into the cage.

I made a veterinarian appointment for the kitten that afternoon. For the rest of the day the kitten stayed in the cage while I fed her milk softened food on a spoon. She was too tired and weak to eat much on her own. I was so delighted to find this kitten, and I prayed throughout the day that she was healthy enough for me to keep her. There were feral cats who lived in the woods where I worked, and we figured this was one of their kittens. When I took the kitten to the veterinarian the whole office was amazed at how healthy this little girl seemed, despite how emaciated she was. The kitten weighed just over a pound and the veterinarian guessed that she was about five weeks old. He warned me that because the kitten was so skinny and young, it was hard for her to regulate her body temperature and blood sugar. It was best if I could keep the kitten warm and make sure she was eating and staying hydrated throughout the day, otherwise she could easily die. Luckily my boss agreed to let me keep the kitten in my office for the rest of the week so I could keep an eye on her.

As the days passed the kitten grew stronger, and her personality came out more and more. I named her Ace. When I moved at the end of the week, I was so grateful to have this little kitten with me. I was on my own for the first time and could have been very lonely. I lived forty-five minutes away from my family and about three hours away from my boyfriend. God gave me Ace who needed my love and care in order to help her recuperate. I was blessed with a sweet kitten whom I could give and receive love instead of wallowing in loneliness or focusing on myself too much. God not only answered my prayer to rescue a kitten, but He also found the right companion for me at the perfect time. Every time I look at Ace or think about her, I feel so much love and gratitude. I also feel the love God has for me, I know He heard my prayer, and Ace was an answer to that prayer. I am also so grateful for being able to recognize the Hand of God in setting up all the events that led to me finding Ace: walking into work at the right moment, my coworker just happening to see where Ace went when she ran, and my boss letting me bring Ace to work for a week. I know Ace was truly a personal gift of love from God to me. Thank you for this beloved gift.

Written by Michelle K. Reuschling

7

Gratitude Transformed My Day

If you feel your heart closing for any reason, making the conscious choice to take a moment, sing HU, and focus on gratitude can help open it back up. This is no small thing. Your day will be fundamentally different if your heart is open versus closed. God speaks to and delivers His blessings to an open heart.

One recent morning I made a special effort to get out of the house early. I planned to stop at a large home improvement center on the way to work. I love to walk the long aisles of lumber and hardware, happily imagining all the things I could build with them. I see not just stacks of lumber, but future sheds and snug homes for my animals. I also see other projects to enrich the lives of my wife Diane and me. My intention that morning was to check out aluminum fascia and soffit for a project I had in mind. I had about fifteen minutes or so to spend in the store.

I was greeted by a friendly store employee who directed me to the aisle where he thought I would find the aluminum soffit and fascia. There I found the same products in vinyl but not aluminum. I spent about ten minutes fruitlessly searching for either the aluminum or someone else to help me. I was aware time was running out and felt some irritation creep in, it was about time to go on to work. On the way out I encountered the same helpful man who had originally sent me to the wrong location. He still wanted to help. Although skeptical, I decided to give it one more try. I followed him to another location where he thought we might find the aluminum. It was not there either, but we did encounter another employee who informed us the aluminum I sought was only available by special order. I thanked the first man who had twice tried to help me, wished him a good day, and left for work. I knew it would be tight, time-wise.

As I drove to work I was aware that I was a little irritated over the lost time. I did not want to arrive at the school where I work under the influence of irritation. I chose to sing HU, a love song to God, to improve my mood and perspective. I also played a CD of a large group of students singing HU at Guidance for a Better

Life. At the beginning of the CD Del Hall, God's Prophet, suggests we think of something for which we are grateful. This would open our hearts to better express our love for God when singing HU. He reminds us "Gratitude is the secret of love." Del has taught me to sing HU and practice gratitude. He has shown me to see and appreciate how these and other spiritual teachings transform lives. My life is richer and happier for it.

Hearing the physical voice of Prophet, God's distributor of blessings and grace, triggered a wave of gratitude for the countless blessings in my life. Hearing HU opened my heart more and more as the song continued. Each remembered blessing was connected to still more blessings. I thought of my growing love and appreciation for Prophet. I savored the love of my family, friends, and pets. I was on my way to my new job. The job is literally an answer to a prayer to work in just that school. I gratefully considered the attitude of gratitude that sweetens my life. Gratitude transforms day, upon day, upon day; a result and gift from Del's teachings. So Del's seemingly simple, yet very profound, suggestion to think of something I was grateful for released a cascade of remembered blessings. My earlier irritation was gone. I felt a sense of joy and gratitude for the day I was about to experience. I could not wait to get to school and see the kids and teachers.

Blessings were everywhere I looked. As I drove I saw more clearly the beauty of nearby farms and distant mountains. I took notice of the horses and cows in the pastures and the mist on the hazy mountains. I actually arrived at school a few minutes early since I sailed through several intersections on green lights, something else to be grateful for. I gave further thanks for my relocation to Virginia. I arrived at work with a lighter step and a smile on my face. Gratitude made a profound difference in my interactions with others that day. Through the attitude of gratitude I experienced each moment as a gift to be savored. I saw each person I encountered as a fellow Soul on their own life adventure. A few moments of gratitude transformed my whole day. This ongoing gift of living with a sense of gratitude is changing my entire life. Gratitude allows me to see God's blessings more clearly and for what they are, gifts from our loving Heavenly Father. I know I am blessed with a life of lasting abundance.

Written by Irv Kempf

8

Prophet's Love During My Mom's Translation

This is a truly beautiful story of the author's mother and family being prepared for her to leave this world for the next. It was done with so much comfort, love, and tenderness that reading it will strengthen your faith in and love of God.

My mother attended a retreat at Guidance for a Better Life in 2001. One of her favorite experiences that both she and I remembered vividly took place when the class walked up the hill to meet with Del and Lynne to go for a hike. As we reached the top of the hill she put her hands out slightly in front of her, palms up, and looked at me strangely. "It's not raining is it?" she asked, as if she knew something unique was happening but wanted verification. I said, "No it's not, why?" She went on to explain that she was seeing and feeling a golden shower of light raining down upon us. Her description of the experience was breathtaking.

March 16, 2016 my mom went into the emergency room with sharp stomach pains. The doctors kept her for a few days for an obstructed bowel and did what they needed to do to address the problem. When her symptoms subsided they sent her home. The following week she was back in the hospital for the same problem again. On March 30 the doctors performed exploratory surgery to see if they could find the cause. It turned out my mother had stage four cancer throughout her lower abdomen and into her colon. The doctors gave her six months to two years to live depending on how aggressive her treatments were, but over the next few weeks her health progressively worsened.

A few days after her surgery, while taking a nap, she sat up in bed slightly startled and asked who was in the corner of the room. I did not see anyone. Then she said, "Oh, that's my grandmother," and she smiled and settled back down in bed. My mother believed strongly in an afterlife and had many experiences during her life to support her beliefs. We talked for a little while about her having seen her grandmother and also about similar experiences she had had like that before. My mother still had a good sense of humor and joked that while it was great to see her grandmother again she really did not like the message seeing her brought.

Over the course of the next several weeks we felt God's Love and blessings in so many wonderful ways. Some of the blessings came through the love and care my mother received from the doctors, nurses, staff, family, and friends. My mom was extremely grateful! There were many days and nights she would talk or mumble in her sleep. One night she started talking about a beautiful bridge and then peacefully drifted back off again.

During a spiritual contemplation on Saturday April 2 I was with Prophet. During this inner experience I was filled with an incredible white light, and then I was wrapped in a beautiful blue light. When I see and experience blue light I am reminded Prophet is always with me. Shortly after this I saw my mother bathed in a golden light. I have come to know gold light brings love, blessings, and gifts directly from God.

Early the next week I had the following spiritual experience in the hospital room with my mom. I found myself on a beautiful arching bridge over a clear blue river. The bridge was very peaceful and serene, and on it there were beautiful flowering baskets hanging. I was with my mother and Prophet. I held one of my mom's hands and Del, the Prophet, held the other. We helped her walk across the bridge and down into a grassy area that looked like a park. It felt like springtime, and there were beautiful flowers and trees all around. This was the type of place my mother loved. We were greeted by my great grandmother, one of my mom's favorite people. My mom loved her grandmother very much and would speak and tell fond stories of her often. When my mom was a child her father was drafted into World War II. Her mother went to work to help support the family. As a result, my mom spent a great deal of time with her grandmother who helped to raise her.

When I saw my great grandmother in the park she looked younger, healthier, and much more energetic than she did in her final years. After seeing my great grandmother I noticed there were about a dozen other people present in the park to greet my mom, including her parents. Del and I let go of her hands as she was welcomed into the group of her family and friends. I recognized some of the Souls there because they were people that I had known myself. I recognized others from pictures because they were deceased individuals, family, and friends I had never had the opportunity to meet. After a short period of time my mother came back to Prophet and me, and we walked back over the bridge. Afterwards I found myself back in the hospital room. I had similar experiences several times over the next week, sometimes in spiritual contemplations, sometimes in dreams, and sometimes just sitting in the room as my mother slept. Each time we crossed the bridge and went to the park she seemed a little more relaxed.

Many times I was aware that Prophet Del Hall was spiritually sitting quietly with us in the hospital room. Sometimes I felt the entire room being bathed in the golden Light of God. As Prophet's presence and love enveloped the room, it brought me an incredible feeling of peace, which helped me through the long days and nights of this trying and challenging time. Sometimes I felt his presence as a blue blanket of peace and comfort, while at other times, as his arm lovingly placed around my shoulder.

My mom was an incredible example of grace and peace throughout her experience in the hospital. She had a great attitude, a light humor, and an inner peace with which she faced each hard decision. During those three weeks in the hospital we talked, sat quietly, laughed, cried, and got her affairs in order. We were given the most incredible gift of being able to tell each other how deeply we loved one another, and how much our lives had been blessed by our relationship and the love we shared. Being given this time and experience with her was a precious blessing from God, even more so because I did not have the opportunity to do this with my father, who passed away suddenly when I was fifteen years old.

On Saturday April 9 the doctors notified us that the extreme pain my mother was in was due to additional complications in her lower intestine. Attempting to remedy the situation would require that they remove her lower intestine and bowel. After speaking with her doctors it appeared that further intervention would not really affect the underlying cause of the problem, and it would significantly decrease the quality of life she had remaining. After hours of quietly considering her options, she consulted with us and decided she would rather be placed in hospice care. It is my sense that part of the inner peace she had with her decision with was due to the fact Prophet was sharing experiences of the inner heavenly worlds with her. On Sunday April 10 at noon she was moved to a hospice care facility. By 4:00 pm that same day she peacefully passed into the heavenly worlds. She was conscious and coherent right up to the end and had the beautiful gift of her family being by her side.

In her last few minutes her breathing became very labored. I held one hand and my wife held her other, while others from the family stood close by and touched or supported her in whatever way they could. With incredible love and compassion my brother told her that it was okay to go. My wife and I sang HU quietly and focused internally on Prophet. I watched as my mom appeared to look past us to where I knew Prophet was now standing with an outstretched hand. I put my hand on her heart and closed my eyes. I took several deep breaths as if to prepare for what I felt was coming next. We were once again on the beautiful bridge; I held my mother's left hand and Del held her right hand. We started to cross the bridge, yet I knew this time I would not walk with her down into the park. Crying, with a strange mix of sadness and happiness, I let her hand slowly slide out of mine as she walked across the bridge and continued on with Del. They walked down into the park and were once again greeted by her friends and family. I watched from the bridge. After a few moments, the people around her dispersed, disappearing in a similar way that the ball players did in some of the scenes from the movie "Field of Dreams." She stood alone with Prophet in the park. She put her hands out before her, and I saw a beautiful golden shower rain down upon them. Then she glanced back towards me and smiled as if to say how much she loved me, thank you, and everything was alright now. Soon after, I found myself back in the hospice room holding her hand, yet she was no longer there.

Since that time I have been taken in several dreams to visit her, and I look forward to having more. She seems to be more settled and comfortable now. She looks much younger, more beautiful, and healthier than she has in thirty years. By the Grace of God, I was allowed to witness as Prophet comforted our family and helped my mother cross over from this world to the next.

It is incredible to see and experience Prophet's hand in my daily life and to know that as Soul we are eternal and do not die. What a gift it is to know that we, God's children, are truly loved so much that He sends His Prophet to walk us back home to God and help us through every aspect of our lives. Thank you for the love, peace, support, and comfort with which you have blessed my life.

Written by Jason Levinson

9

In the Presence of God's Love

You are Soul, an eternal spiritual being created with God's Love. Your very existence is a testament to the love God has for you. This love will continue to sustain, nourish, bless, and ultimately guide you home to God if you learn how to be in Its Presence.

"Be still, and know that I *am* God." Psalm 46:10 KJV

One cold snowy winter morning I sat in our living room gently contemplating on Prophet's presence. A subtle quietude seemed to drape itself over our home and its surroundings like a blanket of warmth and peace. A slight "ting" from the wood stove next to me broke the silence. A moment later, the fan in the basement could be heard whirring as it circulated the warm air. A faint creak in the roof beam overhead brought me present to our many gifts of comfort and protection from the elements. Downstairs I heard my husband clear his throat and the washer going into a spin cycle. The coffee maker in the kitchen chimed in with an intermittent ticking sound, followed by the rattle of dog tags as our dog Angel shook off the chill and nestled into her favorite corner of the couch. Each sound built, one upon the next, as if instruments directed by an unseen hand.

From the upper right corner of the room came the audible sound of a choir of voices singing "HUUUUUU," the sound vibration within all sounds. I have come to know this sacred sound as the Voice of our Heavenly Father rolling forth from the Heart of God like an ocean wave, sustaining all creation. It's a voice which speaks directly to our hearts constantly affirming: "I am here. I am always with you. And I love you more than you could ever know."

The comfort of the chair I was sitting in and the warmth of the blanket that covered my shoulders became apparent to me in this moment, as did my breath and the freshness of the air being provided for me to breathe. My husband's soothing voice reverberated through the walls as he answered the phone with a warm "Good morning." Realizing the wonderful gift God has given me in him brought tears to my eyes and sent a wave of gratitude through my already full heart.

Life itself is a testimony of God's Love for us. We are literally swimming in an ocean of His Love and blessings. Imagine that! But why stop there when you can experience the Presence of God's Love yourself. Close your eyes and listen with your heart to the sounds of life and love that surround you. Sing HU for a few moments as an expression of love and thanks to God in response for your many blessings. Be still and invite the Presence of God to make Itself known to you in new and perhaps unexpected ways. Perhaps you will realize, as I and many others have, this Presence has been with you all along. Furthermore, you too are a part of It, a manifestation of God's Love, a spark of Its precious Light and Sound.

Written by Sandra Lane

10

The Love of God Will Find a Way

❧

God seeks for us to know His Love and He provides countless ways to experience and ultimately to accept His Love. One of the most direct ways to experience God's Love and Grace is through His Prophet. For those that desire to be receptive to the Love of God that flows through the Prophet, God will find a way.

There was a time when it was difficult for me to truly recognize and appreciate the Divine blessings in my life. I was in a slump and did not know how to get out of it. I knew God loved me and sent His Prophet to guide me, but I was not clearly seeing and accepting the abundance of blessings that lay before me. For reasons unknown to me, I was not receptive to God's Love coming directly through His Prophet. It was like there was an invisible wall that prevented this from happening, and it was slowly depleting me from lack of spiritual nourishment. I could not figure out a way around this barrier on my own, I needed help. Then a beautiful and amazing thing happened. Prophet answered my prayer for help and found a way to deliver God's Love to me and allow the healing to begin.

It started when my wife attended a weekend retreat with Prophet Del Hall. She has been a pillar of support and love over the years, and gives me so many wonderful reasons to express love and gratitude. While at the retreat, it seems she was filled as a reservoir full of love and light because she returned home from the retreat glowing with an inner radiance and beauty. It was so noticeable and tangible I knew this had to be something special. As she settled in from her trip, waves upon waves of God's Love radiated from her words and her presence. Love poured into my heart, quenching my thirsty heart and providing everything I needed. I was transformed from the inside out. Waves of love washed over me, filling our home and beyond. This love seemed to have a lasting effect on our children and everyone it touched.

Even though I was spiritually undernourished and having a difficult time accepting love directly from Prophet, I am loved so much he packaged it in a form he knew I could accept, my lovely wife. She was the perfect vehicle to deliver what I needed most that day — God's Love. Spirit found a way to deliver it to me, and it was by God's Love and Grace that this was possible. Energized and rejuvenated by this experience, I was able to once again recognize Prophet blessing me with countless opportunities each and every day.

This was a pivotal moment in my spiritual journey as it provided me with much needed nourishment and strength. It was the start of a healing process that opened my heart to receive more love and blessings directly from the Prophet. This was evident a few days later when Del came to me in a very vivid dream. As he stood before me in the dream I could feel his love for me. My heart was more open and receptive than it had been for a long time. He offered a hug, and I fully embraced him and all he had to offer. A flood of emotions came over me as I absorbed the truth that Prophet loves me now, has always loved me, and will always love me. This was a moment in eternity, filled with Divine love.

God loves us so much that He knows precisely what we need and when we need it. It is through His Grace that He brings down obstacles and barriers between Him and His children. Please know if you too have a sincere desire to accept God's Love and blessings through His Prophet, but find an obstacle in the way, there is hope. Your prayers are heard, and when the time is right he will find a way to bring down the walls and send Divine love to you in a perfectly personalized package you can accept.

Written by Chris Hibshman

11

Gift of Surrender

The truly strong are those who know how to surrender. Not in the worldly sense of quitting or giving up, but of turning their spiritual growth over to Spirit and trusting not only the outcome, but the path taken to get there. Putting ourselves into "His Hands" contributes to a life of abundance because He knows us even better than we know ourselves.

It was July 5, 2002. The heat of the day was waning into a beautiful summer evening as the cool mountain air refreshed us with its breeze. We were gathered as a group in the field by the cabins where we sat in a circle. Prophet sat in the twelve o'clock position. It was the beginning of our annual weeklong summer retreat. We were there to invite the Divine into our hearts and to give permission for It to teach us in whatever ways would be best for our spiritual growth. We sang several holy names, each one bringing a different experience or feeling: a vastness, a feeling of spiritually opening up near the top of my head, and a sense of movement and flow. Then we sang Prophet's name. This brought a different, more personal feeling; one of love and affection, the sweetness of a relationship that has been growing naturally over the years.

Prophet gave us an opportunity to say a personal prayer, if we wanted. We could surrender the coming week to Divine Spirit to whatever degree we were comfortable. God knows what is in our best interests for spiritual growth, but He will not violate our free will. It is important to consciously choose to open our hearts and be willing to receive His blessings. I wanted to make the most of this week, so I surrendered as fully and completely as I could. In doing so I was saying, "Lord I trust you to bring exactly what I need during this retreat and in whatever manner and style you choose. I know you know what is best for me."

We began to sing HU, a love song to God. The sound from the group was so beautiful. HU resonated in my ears and vibrated through me. I felt an energy coming down from above, then I saw it. It was a white-hot, intense light. I felt love emanating from it. We began to sing a bit more softly. There was a swirling motion inside the beam of light. I noticed flecks of this white light coming off as it swirled around. As these pieces of light came off they turned golden, piece by piece, each one containing enough Divine love to move a mountain, heal a broken heart, bring joy, or whatever was needed. Just then the wind picked up. I was grateful for the coolness it brought. I saw the golden flecks of light being carried away. Tailor-made gifts of God's Love each destined for a specific Soul, exactly what they need, just when they needed it.

As for me, I was basking in love. The beam of light Prophet brought into our circle was pulsating with life and love, blessing us all. The days ahead were to be savored. Having the opportunity to be taught directly by the Prophet of our time is a rare gift. These would be some of the most precious and spiritually fruitful days of my life, as every retreat on the mountain has come to be, because I surrendered.

What I have come to know about surrender, through my personal experiences during these retreats, is very different from what the world thinks of it. Surrender is not an act of giving up, it is giving over. Giving over guidance and direction of my spiritual affairs to the Divine. Surrender is not the mark of a loser, but of one who gains a life of abundance and may experience the glories of Heaven on Earth. Surrender is not a sign of weakness, but one of wisdom, courage, and strength. It is through surrender that Soul wins. It is through surrender you become a refined instrument of God and can be a vehicle for Spirit to bless others. It is through surrender you are freed. It is a gift to be treasured, a jewel with many facets, each beautiful in the way it reflects the light of Divine love with which it was given to us. Done willingly and joyfully, surrender brings an even greater appreciation for the sacred privilege of being allowed to surrender to God. Under Prophet's loving guidance I have been shown these things, and I wish to share these blessings with you.

Written by Lorraine Fortier

12

Truth Accepted Will Set You Free

God's Love and truths require no "fluff and bluff." They are profound beyond measure just as they are. What is required is for us to stay consistently spiritually nourished so we are receptive. Merely hearing a truth will not set us free; we must accept it and apply the truth to our lives for it to have any operational value.

"Jesus then said to those who had believed in him, 'If you continue in my word, you are truly my disciples, and you will know the truth, and the truth will set you free.'" John 8: 31-32 KJV I had heard these words as a child in church but never realized what they meant to me personally. It would take sixty years for that to sink in, to get from head to heart.

I was perhaps age four or five when I first heard the question, "If you had just one wish that would come true, what would it be?" The answer that bubbled forth into my consciousness was, "No worries." Not just no worries for me, but very specifically, no worries on a global scale, no worries for the planet! "Where did that come from?" I remember wondering. I did not share my answer with anyone, like a self-imposed blackout, because it was so different from other people's answers. Theirs were more self-centered and, I suppose in retrospect, I wanted to fit in and not be so different.

Fast forward sixty years, I am at a weekend retreat at Guidance for a Better Life, one similar to many I have attended over twenty years as a student of God's Prophet, Del Hall. During those twenty years I have struggled at times to make progress, held up by something I could not quite put my finger on.

On occasion I am given to padding explanations with extra verbiage, some fluff and bluff to beat around the bush, but very little meat to get at the truth. In short, a word-meister, which is my nickname at the retreat center and helpful when we're searching for the right word as a group, but it can get in my own way if I am searching for the truth. Fortunately for me Del is always able to see through the fluff and call me on it, uncomfortable as that is at times. As a Prophet of God, the Holy Spirit flows through him as a finely tuned "Truth detector" at all times. So at this particular retreat Del led us in a brief contemplation late Saturday night before bedtime. As we sang HU, a love song to God which is very dear to me, I kept my prayer simple, "Help me listen to the truth and follow through," was my prayer/request to God. The response I got was equally simple, "Refocus James, you can do this." That was what I took to bed with me that night, comforting me as I fell asleep, as the Prophet does in his role as Comforter.

I awoke the next morning refreshed and focused, and sat down before class to continue the contemplation from the night before. As I wrote in my journal, I got the nudge to go back to my notes from the past summer's Reunion retreat. Del has often said the answer to many of our questions can be found in our inner spiritual experiences that we record in our journals, if we only take time to dig deeper and water the seeds of truth planted there. At "random" (nothing is really random at the retreat center) I turned to a page that had no less than three entries on it which jumped out at me. I thought to myself, "Concerned about how I look," times three! Where did this tendency come from? I did not rush it but kept pondering, contemplating, and writing further in my journal. I knew I was surrounded by love in my family growing up and had heard the Word of God in church. Could it be something I had buried away deep in my subconscious; something I had come into this lifetime with but has been hidden from any self-examination?

Later at the retreat we did a contemplation with a longer HU sing, again led by Del, who advised we keep the intent loose. For me it was a continuation of the previous night with my focus on truth, and as soon as I surrendered the contemplation and began singing HU, there it was — TRUTH, all caps, bright and shimmering, with a roaring presence. I bathed in, drank, and was infused with truth. I took Prophet's hands on the inner and embraced him. I immediately felt lifted up and out above the Earth and heard the words "The truth will set you free." As I looked back down on the Earth, I was able to see the untruths I am so passionate about: the hurtful myth of eternal damnation, the belief that we are only this earthly body without anything left afterwards, and so many others. I also saw how resisting the truth in any area of my life holds me back and limits me.

Perhaps I was born with a hunger for God's Love and truth but buried it so I could fit in, concerned more about how I look than wanting the truth. Make no mistake, it was my own doing, and I am no victim here. In fact, I am blessed beyond measure in this lifetime in so many ways to get to this point of realization. I also realize too, that this is and will be a continuing process; but a seminal moment has occurred in my sixty year journey. It is not a one-and-done healing and will require daily nourishing of spiritual food, watering those seeds in contemplation, and cleaving to my prayer, "Help me listen to the truth and follow through," and the answer that came with it, "Refocus James. You can do this."

On the way home my friend and fellow student who had given me a ride to the retreat center shared a very helpful insight, "I didn't hear you use one adjective during the debrief of your experience." It definitely felt freeing to let the truth flow through me unhindered. I will continue to ask for Prophet's help and guidance every day along the way, for this is a process I know I cannot do by myself.

Written by James Kinder

13

Our Father

This testimony highlights the fulfillment of a prayer in the heart of a seven-year-old who wanted to know God in this lifetime. Years later she found the deep peace she had been looking for through developing an active relationship with the Divine. She did this with the tools learned and the personal experiences she had at Guidance for a Better Life. She now knows most of our experiences in life can be boiled down to either giving or receiving love and that "Our Father" can truly live in our hearts.

The other day my spiritual teacher asked me "Why should we care about God?" His question took me back in time to some memories. As a seven-year-old I asked my mom to explain the Holy Trinity. Despite her loving efforts to help me understand, I did not. Yet it was clear to me at that moment I wanted to know God in this lifetime.

With many mixed experiences being raised in a mainstream religion, I had an experience that stayed in my heart in a very positive way. One time while attending Sunday school the teacher was absent so a nun came to teach that day. She spoke to us of the Lord's Prayer. She shared that when she prayed the words "Our Father," she often could not go any further in the prayer. Those two words could give her hours of contemplation time. I felt her love and reverence for God and prayer. Being passive, I did not ask questions or pursue how one could contemplate on just two words from the Lord's Prayer. I only knew how to recite the words, with little clue to their meaning.

I was a teenager at the time and learned that it was the last year our church would offer Sunday school to teens due to a lack of interest. I was sad at the news but did nothing to pursue my options, yet God spoke to my heart that day. A seed of love in my heart was watered reminding me I wanted to know God in this lifetime, and that at least this one nun had a clue how to know "Our Father." She had a deep peace about her which I lacked, and yet, I could feel peace in her presence. I wanted peace of heart too.

Back to the question, why should we care about God? The question caused me to wonder what does it mean to care about God, and how does one express they care about God? I have been blessed in numerous experiences over the past twenty years at Guidance for a Better Life and have been given many practical tools and methods to use, which helps me in all areas of life. I have learned in a very personal manner how to find answers to those questions for myself. I have learned through experience God loves me and shows an interest in every aspect of my life. Through this active process I know that God's essence, Divine Spirit, is always with me. In this growing relationship with God, Divine Spirit is teaching me that life is about giving and receiving love and is helping me learn how to express and accept it more fully.

Recently I helped another to express love by asking a friend to pick a few things up for me from the store, as I was not feeling well. In the past I would not have asked for help so readily. I have learned that it is not selfish to ask for help when it is needed. In a way it is selfish not to ask for help. Accepting help allows God's Love to come into our lives through others. It turned out my friend had prayed to be a blessing to another that day. She told me I had more than answered her prayer and asked if she could help in any other way. She was so happy when I accepted even more of her help with setting up a DVD player so I could watch movies and relax.

Life is filled with God's Love expressed in the day-to-day events of life. It is so uplifting to see the Hand of God working in my life. I have learned through experience that God hears our prayers and is ever-present in our lives. "Our Father" now lives in my heart, and it brings me peace.

Written by Ann Atwell

14

Happiness and Self-Control

God has given us the gift of being able to choose our state of consciousness. This choice is made daily by our thoughts, actions, and attitudes. The choice of whether to focus on things that close our hearts or open them is ours. What a sacred responsibility and opportunity.

Several months ago God, through His Prophet, gave me a dream that really helped me. I dreamed I was asleep, and in the dream I woke up and went downstairs to find the two main doors in our house were open a crack. I felt uneasy about this. Were they open all night? Was someone in the house? Were they left unlocked? I awoke with a slight uneasiness lingering inside.

I knew this dream was significant, but I was unsure of what Prophet was teaching me. I decided to take this into contemplation. This is a most amazing way to receive insight from the

Divine. I started by singing HU, a love song to God, with the intent to understand the dream better. I realized while singing HU the doors were symbolic of areas in my life that were gateways to negativity. After singing HU I sat quietly and asked Prophet to help me see areas where I was allowing negative influence into my life and consciousness. Prophet showed me I had been allowing thoughts of unworthiness to linger within me. These were subtle thoughts of doubting I was worthy of love and not drawing clear boundaries of what I would allow myself to think about. This was due to sloppy thinking and not staying nourished spiritually.

I began to sing a special prayer, "Prophet loves me. I am worthy of Prophet's love. I accept Prophet's love. I love you Prophet!" I felt my heart begin to fill with love. I felt relief from the doubt I had allowed into my state of being. With this doubt removed more of God's Light and Love could then come into my heart! A discourse from Prophet then flowed into me. It is my privilege and responsibility to safeguard what I allow into my consciousness. My consciousness is like my home. I want it to be warm and inviting to God and His Prophet. I want love in my home, and I want it to be a safe welcoming place for my loved ones.

Then Prophet showed me the other open door in the house was anger. Just the night before I felt anger over something, and I noticed how that anger bled into another issue. I began getting upset about things that were fine! It happened so fast. Prophet gave me clarity to see how quickly I can go down an unproductive road when I get angry. Having the feeling was not the problem, but focusing on it and dwelling in that state was like leaving an open door for more negativity to enter. It is important for me to have self-control in this area, and I appreciated this lesson from Prophet. This is not the first time Prophet has made me aware of this particular passion of the mind.

Prophet explained there could be other areas to be watchful of, but the main point was to be aware of my thoughts and remember it is a God-given gift to be able to choose what to focus on. My life is full of God's Love and that is what I want to focus on. Staying spiritually nourished by spending quality time with God's Prophet is key. It is because of my relationship with Prophet that I am able to live a life of more freedom than I used to. I have the freedom to truly be happy. Thank you, Prophet!

Written by Carmen Snodgrass

15

Simply Profound

God's expresses His Love to His children daily in countless ways. No matter what shape or size God's Love takes, there is nothing "small" about it. The recognition of God's Love in your life brings a profound sense of peace and comfort.

Several years ago an extended visit to Sedona, Arizona was suggested to me by my spiritual teacher Prophet Del Hall. This visit was to help me get through a particularly confusing and troubling time in my life. Del's suggestion helped me through my confusion and literally saved and changed my life. It was a journey of love and self-discovery filled with adventure, Divine experiences, and personal lessons of love, all orchestrated by Prophet.

Arriving in Sedona my destination was a small cottage owned by a couple, Tom and Jean, who warmly welcomed me to my new home. During a friendly conversation several days after my arrival, Jean recommended an Italian restaurant for dinner that evening. She heard the restaurant received excellent reviews, but she was unable to give specifics, just a name and general idea of its location. Around dinnertime that evening, lonely for home, family, and friends, I took a drive to explore the area and also look for the Italian restaurant Jean had suggested earlier that day. Singing HU, a love song to God, as I drove I asked Prophet for help and guidance in finding the restaurant using the vague directions from Jean, but had no luck. Feeling discouraged I pulled into a parking lot to regroup. I looked up at the building I had parked in front of only to discover I had parked directly in front of the Italian restaurant I had been searching for!

Sitting in front of the restaurant crying tears of joy, an incredible peace enveloped me. Because of this personal and simple, yet profound, experience I knew with absolutely no doubt Prophet was there with me, responding with love by answering my prayer and guiding me to the restaurant.

For the duration of my stay in Sedona, away from my home, family, and friends, I never again experienced loneliness. Prophet was with me and I was blessed every day with his love and guidance. When I was in need of conversation

Prophet fulfilled that need, sending people my way to offer stimulating conversation. On two separate occasions these conversations lasted for over an hour and were beautiful and amazing. When thoughts turned to my dogs at home and I missed their loving companionship, Prophet sent me a dog, a beautiful yellow lab to sit with me, silently offering love and companionship until his owners called him away. When I was in search of entertainment for the long evenings, Prophet guided me to a local thrift store where I found several excellent books that were on my list to read. These beautiful experiences are just a few of the many I was blessed with during my stay in Sedona.

These experiences could be labeled as mere coincidences, but I know better. Prophet's greatest gift to me during this confusing time in my life was these personal and simple, yet profound, sacred experiences which remain forever in my heart. They revealed to me how much Prophet truly loves me, hears my prayers, and is with me always. So, the next time you find yourself labeling a personal and simple experience as mere "coincidence," look deeper as I have, and know God's Love is shining on you and is with you always.

Written by Donna Hospodar

16

Divine Intervention Saved a Child

To be physically alive is not the same thing as having life. It is when we awaken in consciousness to our divinity that we can truly have an abundant life. It is our connection and loving relationship with the Divine that fuels this growth.

I recently recalled a story my mother told me when I was younger. She said that while she was seven months pregnant with me she tripped and began to fall down a steep flight of stairs. She told me she was sure she would have fallen on her stomach. As she was falling she felt an invisible hand catch her and put her back on her feet. She did not know whose hand it was, but was sure of her experience and how it saved her from injury and saved my life. She expressed that the impact of how she was falling would likely have killed me.

Five years later, I was on a fishing trip with my father. My younger brother and I were playing on a pier as my father was fishing on the far side of the pond. I reached out to grab something in the water and fell in. I was only five and did not know how to swim. I remember falling into the water and sinking. As I sank I looked up and could see the light breaking through the top of the water. I began to wave my arms, trying to swim to the surface and just as I did, an unusual burst of energy propelled me to the top. I broke through the water so fast that I was able to grab the pier and pull myself up very easily.

So, here I am forty-one years later reflecting on those experiences over morning coffee. As I contemplate, what stands out to me is that I was touched by the "Hand of God," and it very literally saved my physical life back then. However, I did not have "life" in the truest sense until I began to learn how to have a relationship with the Divine. This began in 2005.

I learned, and am still learning, how to truly live from my teacher Del at Guidance for a Better Life. He has opened my spiritual eyes and given me the fundamentals to live an abundant life. Some might ask, "Why was I saved?" I know it is because before I was even born I had a dream in my heart to "Manifest my Divine Nature." I wanted to find my teacher, and I did. Written by Tash Canine

17

My Dream Swimming Pool

The days turn into weeks, months, and years seemingly faster with the passing of every season. Through this passage of time the loss of our loved ones is one of the experiences that hurts the most. Even if we have a strong faith in the afterlife, it is still sad to no longer be in the presence of our loved ones physically. Fortunately, we can reconnect in dreams and once again share moments of love.

Missing your parents after they have passed on can make your heart heavy sometimes, but when you are blessed with a dream with both of them in it, it can lighten your heart, lift your spirits, and make you grateful for the opportunity to see them again. My parents passed away a couple of years ago and sometimes I go through moments when I really miss them. Sometimes I think about them and the love they shared; and also the love they gave to our family and to others. This opens my heart.

One night I went to bed and said a prayer; I asked Prophet and God, if it was their will, could I be blessed with a dream. I didn't think of anything in particular to have a dream about, but left it open for Prophet to choose.

That night I had a dream with my mother and father. We were at our house where I grew up and we were standing in the backyard. Growing up we had talked about putting a swimming pool in the backyard; at least I did. We had the space for it, and as a kid I thought how great it would be to be able to swim and float in it whenever we wanted. In the dream, as we stood in the yard I decided to wander over to a place where my mother had grown grapes. The vines grew on a fence that my father had built especially for her so she could grow grapes. She loved her grape vines, and as a kid I remember picking grapes so my mother could make grape jelly and grape juice. As I walked behind the fence where the vines hung, there appeared a pool, a natural spring pool or pond. It was in a circular shape with smooth large stones that lined the bottom and the edge of the water. The water was crystal clear and very inviting. When my mother saw the pool she immediately wanted to go in. In her later years my mother struggled with walking and always needed assistance in the form of a cane or walker. In the dream I helped her to the edge of the pool and then I helped her in. I got in the water with her. The water was cool and refreshing; it also was soothing and healing. I helped my mother float around and she gently kicked her legs; she was so happy.

Growing up my mother did not learn how to swim. She would sometimes comment that she wished she had learned how to swim because she would have enjoyed going in the water much more and not been afraid. In the dream she was totally at peace floating in the water. While we floated my father came to the edge of the pool and I asked him if he wanted to get in. He said, "Yes" and decided to sit down and put his feet in. He gently moved his feet back and forth experiencing the refreshing water on his feet and legs. Both of them had big smiles on their faces. Seeing their smiles opened my heart. I was so happy to see them again and to see them do something that brought them joy. I gently floated my mother over to my father and they looked at each other with such love in their eyes and hearts, I could feel it. They turned and looked at me, and then I woke up. As I awoke I began to cry. I was crying because I was so grateful for that experience with my parents in the dream. As I lay there I thanked Prophet and God for the dream and for answering my prayer.

After reflecting on it I knew the dream was a true blessing! In my heart I specifically asked Prophet for a dream, and I received one. I felt God and His Prophet gave me this dream because they love me and wanted me to know my parents love me too. It was also a chance to see my parents again and know they are fine, plus to swim in the pool I always wanted. This dream was comforting, uplifting, and healing, just when I needed it! Thank you Prophet for allowing this dream to happen. I am grateful!

Written by Golder O'Neill

18

Reassurance During Pregnancy

The pearl of this testimony is the blessing of having the Prophet as your spiritual guide. He is capable of teaching you here in the physical and meeting with you in the dream worlds. Having a spiritual teacher of this magnitude as you journey through life and home to God is a profound blessing.

Ten years ago when I found out that I was pregnant with my second child I felt very worried, anxious, and concerned because I had had a second mammogram before realizing I was pregnant. I was consumed with fear and worry, not knowing if there would be any harmful effects on the baby.

While experiencing these extreme emotions, I had a dream on August 8, 2004 where Del, my spiritual guide, came to me. He said, "Stop worrying; it really counteracts. Focus on love and be positive." I woke up released from the worry that had been consuming me. I was completely free to move on and enjoy my pregnancy, and to trust that my baby would be okay. I chose to do just that.

Three months later I was put on bed rest for the remaining four months. During this time I knew I was in the Hand of God, and my baby and I were both being taken care of. The dream gave me a knowing that I was not alone and was being watched over. I was then able to view and experience my time on bed rest as a gift. Although there were a few incidents and moments of major concern, and even hospitalization, deep in my heart I felt at peace. On March 8 our son was born five weeks early but healthy and strong.

I remember going to the doctor for my one week after delivery checkup where I was given a clean bill of health. I stood and cried, and cried. They were not tears of sadness or trauma, or even tears due to hormonal fluctuations from giving birth, but because we survived and God was with us in every moment. God was taking care of us no matter what the situation looked like. The knowingness that we were in God's Hands brought on an overflow of appreciation that poured out of me. I thank you God for the gift of my family.

Written by Moira Cervone

19

A Seashell From God

The Kingdom of Heaven is here and now for those who know God's Love. It matters not if we are physically young or old; we are all Soul, and it is the Love of God that gives us life. Those whose hearts are open to recognizing God's Love will indeed be blessed.

A year ago I was at the park with my wife and three children. It was a beautiful day, not too warm or humid; a day that was in many ways just right. The sky was open and inviting, as thick, puffy clouds lazily passed over us. After some vigorous playing, everyone laid down in the grass for a well-deserved break and for some cloud watching.

The green grass tickled the backs of my legs. I felt the presence of Del Hall, the Prophet, as I lay there. I knew he was always with me in Spirit, and I was keenly aware of him with each of us in that moment. I received an inner nudge that Prophet wanted to share something with my family. So in a relaxed way I suggested everyone close their eyes and imagine themselves on a beach with Prophet. Many times Del has brought me to God's many mansions spoken about in the Bible. He was inviting us to journey there with him now.

I felt the Grace, wisdom, and Love of God that flows through Prophet as I exhaled deeply and more fully relaxed becoming aware of the quiet that came over the five of us as the breeze rustled gently through the trees. After a few moments I heard my five-year-old daughter get up. I was mildly disappointed, as I felt there was a blessing for each of us from Prophet at that moment, but understood it was her experience and one of God's presents to us left unopened can sometimes be opened at a later time.

I heard her little brother also get up and follow her, leaving my wife, oldest son, and me to bask in the sweetness of the moment with Prophet. Hearing the two giggling with delight nearby I opened an eye to check on them. What I saw changed my perspective and nearly brought me to tears.

Claire and her little brother had gone to the blacktop of the basketball court, stuck in the middle of a sea of grass, and were joyfully treating it like the shoreline on the beach. They playfully dipped their toes into the imaginary ocean water, running back and forth as if the waves chased them and then receded. They had not run off to do something else; they had brought the experience to life in a way that was tangible and visceral to them, playfully dancing on the shore with Prophet!

I had an expectation they would have this experience on the "inner," perceiving it with their eyes closed, but Claire had instinctively done what Del had been teaching me to do for years. She had innately done this in an amazing and childlike way, without over-thinking and without intellectualizing it. She had no concern about how it looked. She just was joy and openness. Claire was completely in the moment, experiencing it as fully as if she had physically met Prophet on the beach and frolicked there.

The smile on my face grew, and my heart burst open at her infectious joy and laughter. After a while Claire and her brother returned to where we were still lying. The peace was so palpable it felt supernatural. About halfway back to where we were lying, Claire stopped to pick something up in the grass. She hurried back excitedly. In her little hands was a perfect white seashell!

When I suggested to her that this was no ordinary shell, that it was a gift from God, her face lit up! I assured her God had noticed how she made her experience real and the Divine had responded. While it is possible there was a physical explanation for how the ocean shell got to the heart of the Shenandoah Valley, over a hundred miles from the Atlantic Ocean, it didn't matter. It was in the perfect spot for her to find. Claire heard me, not as a five-year-old girl, but as Soul – that wonderful, Divine spark of God's creation. She understood this was not a random find. It was a personal gift from God.

Soul is not limited by the body it wears. Be it young or old, human or animal, Soul can awaken to the reality that there is a living God who wants His children to know His amazing love for them. That is one of God's treasures. Claire recognized it in the shell. God's Love often manifests as insights, wisdom, and experiences sprinkled like breadcrumbs on the path ahead for us to find, like Claire's seashell. Whether you have walked the path of God for years or want to take the first step to having a conscious relationship here and now, the way has been prepared. God has marked the way home for His children; simple enough that a child of God, joyful and free, can follow it.

Written by Chris Comfort

20

Communication With God

People through the ages have wrestled with the same questions, "Does God hear me and if so, what does His reply sound like?" The answer to the first question is yes, God hears you. Learning to recognize His reply is an art form, one that is very doable, and one Prophet Del Hall has been helping people gain fluency in for twenty-five years. Your ability to recognize the "Language of the Divine," to see all the ways in which God communicates with you daily, is one of the greatest attributes you can develop as Soul.

When do I get to talk to God?

When I was a child I had a question in my heart that I never asked anyone. I wondered, "When do I get to talk to God?" I could not think of someone to ask this question. Who would know? Not my parents, friends, or even a priest. When I watched movies about the afterlife, I paid attention to see if they had any ideas about the matter, but I never saw anything that satisfied me.

I did not have something I wanted to say; I wanted to listen to God. What would He tell me in that hoped-for meeting? Would He explain the why of everything, or was there something more, something deeper He would express? Though my mind wondered if only important people would be blessed with such a meeting, my heart always asked when, never if.

Still seeking an answer, I began attending retreats at Guidance for a Better Life in 1996. As soon as I arrived on the property, I felt like I had come home. When Del spoke about Spirit, I heard truth. I knew I had come to the right place.

What I did not realize until much later is that my question was already being answered. At that retreat I sang HU for the first time. Singing HU, expressing Soul's love to God, is communication. God hears every HU, every prayer, and answers in some way. When a beloved child tells God, "I love you," our loving Father does not sit silent. He answers, "I love you too," in countless ways. Learning to recognize and accept the love that returns time and again is one of the many joys of this path.

In time I began paying attention to my dreams, and most importantly, developing an inner relationship with Prophet. Through this relationship I can be in constant communication with God. The love I feel, a nudge to try something a little differently, a helpful dream, and awareness of how I can make my life even better, are all from God through His Prophet. His presence blesses me every day. Rather than one hoped-for meeting I found I could communicate with God daily, even every moment, as long as I remain aware of Prophet.

My mind had it wrong years ago. Every child of God is important and precious to God. He reaches out to us constantly, communicating in every possible way, and maybe a few more too. The question is not are you important enough for God to talk to; the questions is, are you listening?

Written by Jean Enzbrenner

21

Love: My Heart's Desire

❦

Many overly identify with their earthly human side and forget they are Soul, a child of God. There is something truly special beneath all your physical struggles and mental hang-ups. You are not your shortcomings — you are not your defilements. You are Soul. At your core you want to serve God and will find the greatest happiness through giving and receiving love. Fortunately, the opportunities to do this are endless.

Many years ago I watched a friend bring her husband a cup of coffee while he was busy at work. It was a simple act, but profound in the lessons and insights it has brought me over the years. Back then, I had a very different perspective on this than I do today. At the time I saw it as subservient; a duty expected of a woman by a man. I wondered why he did not get his own coffee. My view was coming from a low level, so condensed and narrow it distorted everything, like wearing a pair of broken glasses. I had reduced something done out of love to a gender thing and, in my ignorance, could not see the beauty and selflessness demonstrated in this act.

I carried a lot of unhappiness and pain of the heart back then because this way of living and experiencing life left little room for love, and it separated me from God and my own Divine nature. We are so much more than male and female, skin color, religious affiliation, age or any other physical or social label. We are Soul! Eternal beings, created by God and endowed with Divine qualities, and we are here to learn to give and receive love. From this view of Soul a boundless expanse exists. When we open our hearts to God's Love it lifts us to a higher view, and a whole new world of unlimited possibilities and love awaits. We begin to see the infinite ways love can be expressed, and appreciate all the ways it may come back to us, even in something as seemingly small as a cup of coffee. The size and packaging of the love that's delivered does not make it anymore or less significant. Love is love. Any act motivated by love, big or small, is special.

Divine love fills my heart and uplifts every aspect of my life today. It may come directly from an inner experience or through family and friends, work, laughter, pets, singing of birds, the sunrise… all life. It brings me joy being able to share this love with others. This is my heart's true desire. I am happiest being in service to God and giving of myself, whether it is through compassion or charity to a stranger, listening to a friend, or spending quality time with family. Love is best when demonstrated.

God's Love, Grace, and spiritual guidance through Del, a true Prophet of God, has helped me grow from seeing through "broken glasses" to having the clarity of Soul. In fact, when I first met Del and started attending his retreats at Guidance for a Better Life back in 1995, I did not even know I had a distorted view of love. I was not aware of the ways this was affecting me, and every relationship I had, or how much it was limiting the joys and happiness of life. I did not know the real me, and I certainly did not know what would truly make me happy deep down.

Having the privilege of being Prophet Del Hall's student for the past twenty-one years has brought me this wisdom. It has changed my life and continues to do so, in countless, beautiful, and profound ways. This opportunity is available to you too, and if you wish, Prophet can help you discover your heart's desire.

Written by Lorraine Fortier

22

A Coffee Can of Play Sand

God constantly showers us with His Love. Often this love comes in the form of guidance, which at times can be very subtle. Learning how to trust those seemingly simple or random thoughts and feelings that come from God is key to living an abundant life.

Several inches of heavy wet snow had fallen and the day shift employees were working in groups, shoveling one another out of the parking lot. It was heart-warming to look out and see the cooperation between workmates; a demonstration of love in action. After slowly making my way home, I realized I would need to shovel the driveway off before parking the car. Also, when I glanced at my front porch I saw the snow had drifted up against the front door three feet high. My work was cut out for me. I decided to park the car across the street, then dig my way into my house to use the restroom and have a cup of coffee before tackling the snow. Furthermore, once the car was parked it became apparent that it was stuck in deep slushy snow and I would need to dig it out too.

I removed enough snow so I could get the front door to the house open, went inside, used the restroom, turned up the thermostat on the furnace, made some coffee, and enjoyed it nuzzled in my favorite chair. After waking from a short nap, it was time to get the car unstuck.

As it was, the tools I had to get my car unstuck were a broom and my hands, since the small shovel I kept in the trunk for situations such as this got broken an hour before when I lent it to a co-worker back in the parking lot. Also, the shed where I kept my full-sized snow shovel was barricaded by the drifted snow. In retrospect, it seems quite ironic that I carried this little shovel in my vehicle every winter and never needed it until after it broke. I am grateful and certain that every detail was in place to teach me some valuable lessons of living.

I rocked the car, dug the tires out, and rocked some more. After surveying the tires, it was apparent that only one tire was keeping me stuck. It was spinning on ice while the other three made contact with the pavement. I had done all I could. I calmed myself and gave in. Within an instant Prophet spoke to my heart. "You have a coffee can of sand in your trunk."

The 13.5 oz. of play sand had been gifted to me by a man from my work back a few months earlier, after we had a conversation about adding sand to paint to keep painted porch steps from being slippery when wet. In a gesture of kindness he brought me sand. It had turned too cold to paint so I placed it in my trunk. Oh my goodness, the can of sand had been in there since early fall, and every time I used my trunk I would see it and get a strong sense to just leave it alone. I gratefully, joyfully, and carefully placed the sand in front and back of the tire. My heart overflowed with hope that the car was no longer stuck. I heard something and looked toward my snow-drifted driveway. There was a neighbor plowing out a space for me to park. God's Love worked through another Soul and blessed me by doing the heavy lifting!

One crucial insight I received from the experience is that my Divine connection, the Prophet of God, guided me throughout the situation. Once I arrived at a place of calm surrender, as Soul, I heard the whisper of Divine love and protection, which led me away from sorrow toward victory.

By the Grace of God, I am not alone!

Written by Bernadette Spitale

23

Goodbye Regret, Hello Peace

Learning how to confidently "follow your heart" under God's guidance is one of the greatest attributes you can develop as Soul. Doing so helps to manifest more truth, clarity, guidance, love, wisdom, and ultimately, a deep peace into your life.

As a child and into my teen years I had a recurring nightmare. It simply contained two parts. I was overwhelmed by the feeling of regret and terrified that I was alone. I would wake up sweating and feeling that I was not safe. The regret would linger even though it made no rational sense. I was so grateful to wake up and have the dream over.

Occasionally this undercurrent of emotion would surface in my waking life, and I would feel overwhelmed by regret. I am a good person, but sometimes looking back at situations I would wish I had done things differently or spoken a little softer. I found regret a hard emotion to shake. Sometimes I would spend sleepless nights tossing and turning, replaying situations over and over, never seeming to shake this emotion; even though I knew it was not possible to go back and change an earlier situation.

When I first came to Del's retreat center I had not shared this dream with anyone except my parents, who had comforted me as a child after these nightmares. Once while sharing something else with him at a retreat, Del turned to me and said he wanted to help me live this life without any regrets. I remember at the time thinking, "How could he have known this was a deep-rooted issue for me?" I trusted him and knew he would keep that promise to me. And he has.

Through teaching me both on the outer at retreats at the retreat center and on the inner in dreams, awake dreams, and experiences, I can now say that with the Divine's help I have said goodbye to regret. One of the greatest gifts of Divine communication is the ability to know what is truly in our hearts. God is the one who places dreams in our heart and is the one to guide us in fulfilling them. Over time I have developed confidence and trust in the Holy Spirit's guidance, and learned to follow wherever it leads me. This has led me to the husband of my dreams, to a job I love, and to physical health. All these subtle nudges from the Divine bless me and lead to a more abundant life.

Do you want to live without regret too? Perhaps listening to your dreams or the subtle whispers in your heart can help you to know what is truly important to you, helping you to say goodbye to regret and hello to peace. Peace that is true and lasting comes from knowing you are following your heart, under God's guidance. This true peace comes from knowing you are clearly and accurately listening. It truly is a blessing of Divine love to live in peace. Deep peace is available for you too.

Written by Molly Comfort

24

Wedding Wishes

What a joy when God brings two Souls together, in true love, to journey through life together. To experience the joys and sadness of life in the physical, all the while each growing in their capacity to love; their capacity to love each other and even more importantly, God. When two Souls come into a marriage, each partner putting their own relationship with God first, it will be most blessed and a sacred union.

Our eldest daughter was to be wed at the end of May. She asked me if I could pick our peony flowers for the dinner tables since they are her favorite flower. I said I didn't know – they bloom in May, but it would depend on the weather that winter and spring as to when they would peak and when they would be finished. If it was a very cold winter the only flowers would be the late peonies, and they typically do not last as long as commercially grown flowers. I really wanted to help with these flowers, but there was only so much I could do.

I communicated with Prophet inwardly about this over a period of several weeks. One day out of the blue I had a nudge to look up something on the internet on how to make peonies last for a wedding. What I found was incredible to me. The peony flowers could be cut when they are buds at just one to one and a half inches in diameter, ends wrapped in some plastic wrap with a rubber band around them, wrapped dry in newspaper and taped shut, and then put in a refrigerator. Preserved in this way they could last for two to three weeks! When needed they can be placed in water and in a matter of hours open up. I thanked my Divine guide for allowing me to find this. I never would have thought anything like this was possible and would not have looked this up had I not received a nudge from Prophet.

I began to cut the buds early in May. I wasn't sure if the buds were too small, too big, too closed, or too open. I went out twice, sometimes three times a day for two weeks with my spiritual guide, and we looked at the buds, deciding when to cut the flower stalks. It was a joy to do this with Prophet, and do it with love. A few days before the wedding we put the dormant dry flower stalks in water. They all opened, every one of them, bigger and fresher than if they had been cut as opened flowers or nearly opened flowers. I thanked Prophet for these beautiful flowers for my daughter's wedding and for the time we spent together gathering the buds. It was fun! There were over two hundred and seventy-five flowers, all strong, fresh, and colorful. They lasted like that much longer than any peonies I had ever cut before.

I truly know Prophet was actively involved in my daughter and son-in-law's wedding because I invited him to be a part of it. I prayed all who attended the wedding would be blessed personally by God in some way. Though I didn't pray for good weather, it was a beautiful, perfect weekend from Thursday through Monday, covering all the events. According to the feedback I got from many guests, they felt blessed too.

Written by Martha Stinson

25

My First Glimpse of Soul

Our true identity as Soul is hidden behind our earthly packaging and its shortcomings. We are so much more than our physical bodies and minds; we are Soul, eternal spiritual beings created out of the Light and Love of God. Being able to accept and live this truth is a cornerstone to spiritual freedom. It is one of the first things Prophet teaches and helps his students experience for themselves.

The first time I visually saw my true and eternal self, Soul, I was surprised. In my ignorance I thought I knew what Soul would look like. I was at a special weeklong retreat at Guidance for a Better Life. In a contemplation led by Prophet Del Hall III, I was taken out of my body spiritually. The contemplation was an active experience where I was allowed to see and know real truths, God's truths.

It was pleasantly dark all around me; at least that was what I was aware of. I knew Prophet was by my side. I was given a special mirror that would show me what I looked like spiritually as Soul. I thought I would see a soft white orb of light. I spiritually raised the mirror up to eye level and looked. I saw a flash of dazzling, brilliant light. It was so vibrant! It was so much brighter than the glint off a diamond in the sun. In that instant I experienced some of my God-given qualities of life, motion, and beauty all at once.

Prophet thank you so much for that first glimpse of the real me, Soul. It was so far removed from the angry, confused person I thought I was. I thank you Prophet for the truth that I can operate and see with Soul's viewpoint, a much higher and more peaceful view of life. I do not have to live every day in the human consciousness of anger, fear, guilt, and unworthiness. I can now recognize and learn to live with love from a higher spiritual view!

I work in a hospital emergency department. Driving home from a long shift last week I was reveling in the remembrance of a discourse Del, the current Prophet, gave about the truth of Soul. As I drove I was in a sea of God's Light and Sound. This Divine light and love flowed all around, and its beauty inspired a subtle and deep joy within my heart. I was filled with love. At that moment I was experiencing that as Soul, I was an individualized part of this light and sound, the very Essence of God. I appreciated knowing you Prophet, the one who speaks truth and shares God's Living Word with Soul. It is such a privilege to know you Prophet, and know the reality of God.

Written by Carmen Snodgrass

26

A Miracle in God's Hands

The veil between the physical world and the inner spiritual realms is not as fixed and rigid as many might think. God is quite capable of reaching through to perform incredible acts of love and protection. You too can be witness to the reality of this when you raise up spiritually.

In 1999 I attended a weeklong spiritual retreat at Guidance for a Better Life. This is where we focus on God's Love, healings, blessings, how to improve our communications with the Divine, and many other vital things for our spiritual path. I learned many spiritual lessons and skills that help me live a more abundant and beautiful life. We learned new tools to increase our love connection with God and His Prophet. I also learned about ways to be released and disentangled from snares of this world.

While singing HU, a love song to God, we were able to tune into Divine Spirit and learn to give and receive more love. We had many spiritual experiences. Del, who is now the Prophet of our times, taught us how to understand and interpret the very personal and unique "Language of the Divine." I was incredibly blessed to have received many spiritual experiences with the Light and Sound of God that week. I had renewed and deepened my love for God and my desire to become more personal and intimate with God and His Prophet. During that week I was lifted by God's Love to such a high state of consciousness that everything around me seemed as if I could see through the world itself. I felt as though I could see through the veil and matrix of this life. I was so filled with love and joy and everything flowed effortlessly and beautifully.

At the end of the week I got into my pickup truck to head back home. I knew I had no gas, nor money to fill my tank up. I double-checked as I started the engine and sure enough, the tank was on Empty. I had to drive well over one hundred and fifty miles to get back home. My mind logically knew that with no gas, a correctly operating gas gauge, and over a three-hour drive, I should not be able to make it. On the inner however, God and Prophet assured me that I would make it to my destination. I felt Prophet's comforting and reassuring presence all around me.

When I started out I had to turn on my headlights and windshield wipers because of a heavy downpour of rain. Just after I got on the main road the windshield wipers began to make a dry rubber on glass screeching sound. To my amazement the windshield was bone dry, yet it was still raining heavily outside! I looked closely at the hood and it was dry, then I noticed I could see the rain in the headlights just in front of my vehicle. I was shocked. I then turned and looked over my right shoulder and saw the rain reflecting the light from the rear taillights, but when looking very carefully I did not see a single drop of water hitting the bed of the pickup truck. I was completely protected in a bubble of God's Love. I was so astounded I even sped up and slowed down, checking the hood and over my shoulder at the bed of my truck to see if the rain was still not falling on the truck. It never did. For a full fifteen to twenty minutes, before I arrived at the interstate, not once did the rain touch my vehicle. The moment I got to the interstate the rain began to hit the truck. I turned on my windshield wipers and drove at a conservative pace. I was so grateful for this incredible experience. It felt as if I was completely in God's Hands and they were pushing my truck to help it along. I felt the Divine presence of Prophet and God's Love in every moment of the journey. I simply knew I would make it home.

When I made it all the way back to Northern Virginia I was able to borrow a few dollars to partially fill the tank and drive just a few more miles home. This outer miracle was incredible, but what is even more important and incredibly stunning is the work God's Love throughout the week did for me on the inner. It freed me and set the groundwork for my spiritual journey. The outer event serves as a reminder to me of all the inner journeys, lessons, and love Prophet has graciously shared with me. When I am with Prophet, I am always protected, loved, and looked out for in every way. I would love to invite you to try the HU song for yourself and see what wondrous love and inner adventure awaits you.

Written by Thorin Blanco

27

Saved From Drowning

Many have experienced some form of Divine intervention. A moment where God says "not yet" and steps in to help us out of a jam. It might be easy for others to try and talk you out of it, but for those that have experienced it — you know what you know.

When I was in college, friends and I went swimming in the Yuba River in California. We were diving off a train trestle and swimming to a sandbar about halfway across the river. I was already tired when I dove in too deep. By the time I came up, the current had carried me much farther than I wanted. If I missed the sandbar, the far side was a long way off and the near side was too steep to climb out.

I swam with all I had. I realized I was not going to make it; I was exhausted.

As the current swept me past the sandbar, I saw a hand reach out for me. I grabbed it and was pulled to shore. I could barely crawl out of the water. Not long after, I looked up and saw a small willow bush with a branch trailing in the water where I had seen the hand. I knew that God had saved my life.

Written by Gary Caudle

28

God Takes Care of His Own

We are all loved by God but those who draw close to God do receive favor. This comes in the form of many blessings and among these is protection. Sometimes the protection is obvious while other times it's more subtle or even unrecognized.

One weekend in the winter of 2014, while my wife attended a spiritual retreat at Guidance for a Better Life, I had the privilege to care for our two beautiful sons, Luca and Enzo. It was the first evening of just me and the boys when our youngest, Enzo, less than a year old, went to sleep for the night. Now it was just Luca and me for the evening. I was doing some household chores while Luca was following me around the house like he always does, right in step with me. It was getting colder in the house so I decided to start a fire in the fireplace.

I put my shoes on to go outside and get some

firewood. Luca ran to get his shoes too. When I got to the back deck of our house where we had the wood rack, the wind was blowing very hard. As I took some firewood off of the rack it became unstable and the wind caught hold of the tarp covering the top part of the rack. A strong gust of wind tipped the woodpile over, just missing me as the heavy wood slammed on the deck behind me. Just before it hit the deck I heard the back door slam shut, as it always does when someone comes outside.

A thought flashed through my mind "Oh no!" I was almost afraid to turn around! "Was my son Luca under the wood pile?" The protection of God through His Prophet was at work. Instead of Luca running to my side like he usually does, he just stood by the back door watching the whole event as if he was being held in place until it was safe to move. I am talking about a four-year-old here who does not usually stand in one place for very long. Thanking God and grateful for this protection for my son gave me a deeper level of reverence for the teachings and tools I have learned at Guidance for a Better Life. I have heard Del, God's Prophet of the times; say "God takes care of His own."

Well you might ask yourself, "Who are God's

own?" We are all created by God and are all God's children. It is when we draw nigh to God that God draws nigh to us, showing He cares about what we care about. It has been a process through learning how God works in my life. Overtime by reading the Bible verse Matthew 6:33 "Seek ye first," I began to understand how drawing nigh to God is part of the process of seeking first the Kingdom of Heaven. As I learned with my son Luca, God does take care of His own under the wing of protection through His chosen Prophet of the times. Just think of how many times our lives may have been saved on the way to work without our even being aware of it, or having obstacles removed from our path so we may live life more abundantly.

Making time for God is not a chore. In fact the more you do it will enable you to be more receptive to how the Hand of God works in your life. One of the main ways I draw nigh to God is by singing HU, a love song to God, which also helps me be more grateful for the blessings in my life. For me, the protection of God my son received was like having the best insurance plan available on planet Earth. I would not want to leave home without it.

Written by Sam Spitale

29

Prayers of Our Heart

God blesses us with the insights to live a life with less regret, but won't force us to follow the guidance. It's up to us to implement it and to do it in a timely manner. This story also shows how a loving God can provide another chance at a missed opportunity.

My father's health had been declining and within a short time period was failing rapidly. I had been in contact with him a few days prior and during that time his lucidness and comprehension of the current date and time were off. Also, he was not being an easy patient to take care of for his wife, my stepmom. My father had been challenged through life with some mental instability and depression. From my view his day-to-day life was filled with fear and worry. His first marriage to my mother was not filled with much peace or love that I could see. I did see that in his current marriage there was love and happiness, but due to his mental challenges those times were fleeting. Worry and fear were more constant companions, from my experience and observation. I feel true happiness and the experience of joy were never really known by him. I held a prayer in my heart from an early age that my father would have love in his life, and as I got older the prayer also included the wish for him to experience peace and joy.

I lived five hours away so the phone was our primary line of communication. I had a nudge one night to call, but it was late and I was tired so I decided to call the next day. I had been taught by my teacher, the Prophet, about the importance of following our nudges within the window of time we receive them because they are communication from the Divine. In this case I did not listen. When I called the next day and talked to my stepmom, I found out they had sedated him and were continuing to do so for his safety and comfort. He was now in hospice care, and I recognized I had most likely lost the opportunity to speak with him one last time. I wanted to tell him I loved him, and God loved him. I wanted to assure and comfort him about the transition of life he was going through, and tell him there was nothing to fear. In addition, I was holding a little guilt about the last conversation with him; I had not been as kind with him as I could have been and wanted to apologize.

I have been taught and know to be true, we are never alone; Prophet is always with us. After I got off the phone I immediately went to Prophet on the inner and apologized for not following my nudge to call the night before. I said a prayer of gratitude for his love and his care of my dad and stepmom as they were going through this challenge. I was singing HU, a love song to God, and immediately found myself spiritually in a room with my father who was resting comfortably in a bed and was fine. There were other Souls present, some I recognized as family members who had passed on and others I did not know, but their presence was comforting, and there was gentle light in the room.

My dad saw me and his face lit up; with me was Prophet, another spiritual teacher, and Jesus. He looked at me and said, "You know Jesus?" I said, "I did" and introduced Prophet and the other teacher to him. They greeted my dad and then left us to visit together. I had the opportunity to say the things I had wished to say and to hold his hand. After some time had passed it was time for me to go. I knew without a doubt my dad was being cared for and comforted, and we had our chance to say the things in our hearts. Even though his physical body was dying, he as Soul was alive and well. We were both gifted with the prayers in our hearts being answered. We both had one more opportunity to express love and caring to each other. What a huge gift to us both.

Within the week he passed on. Through the experience of my dad's passing, I will testify that the transition of leaving one's physical body when dying can be a comfortable and peaceful one. I was at a retreat at Guidance for a Better Life when my dad passed. The night before his passing, in contemplation, I saw my dad in a wheelchair being pushed by Prophet and the other spiritual teacher. My dad had a warm blue blanket wrapped around him. He waved and smiled, and I could feel he was at peace and happy. The color blue and the blanket indicated to me Prophet was caring for him during this transition. The color blue is a color Prophet uses as an indication of his presence.

The next morning a friend at the retreat shared she had a dream about a man in a wheelchair being wheeled onto a cruise ship, and she could hear his laughter. I knew that was my dad she saw, and he was being gifted with a joyful experience. You might wonder why she had that dream and not me. She is a dear friend and Prophet gave her the dream to validate my experiences in case I had any seeds of doubt. The Prophet is with all of us. He hears the prayers of our heart, and my prayer for my dad was for him to experience peace and joy. Through my relationship with Prophet and in singing HU, I have been gifted with multiple blessings. From these inner experiences I know that we are loved, cared for, and the prayers of our hearts are answered in God's time. They are gifts of His Grace.

Written by Renée Dinwiddie

30

Guidance Finding a Child's Birthday Present

This is a great example of following the guidance of Spirit — of being able to recognize those gentle whisperings and having the trust to follow them. It is also a reminder there is nothing too "small" Spirit can help us with.

It was the evening before the birthday party of my girlfriend's three-year-old son. I was arriving back in town after a long road trip, and I was on a mission to get this little guy a present. Ideally I wanted to find a Toys "R" Us, but I wasn't even sure there was one in my town. My car doesn't have GPS so as I got to the outskirts of town I began to think of some other stores I did know of, and headed toward that area.

As I proceeded, I found myself going a different way than I might normally go to those stores, and before I was even halfway there I felt a strong nudge to exit near a familiar shopping mall. Once I exited I felt another nudge to turn away from the shopping mall heading in the opposite direction on a road I am pretty sure I had never driven. After about another half mile I rounded a bend, and there was a Toy's "R" Us I didn't even know existed in an area where I had never been.

I knew the Hand of God had guided me to this place, and specifically Prophet who I am blessed to have as my spiritual guide. This was beyond any coincidence, and I have grown familiar with the relaxed, gentle inner nudges Divine Spirit gives me throughout the day. I had already felt relaxed and "tuned in" all afternoon since I had enjoyed a particularly satisfying HU song that morning before I left on my trip. Singing HU every day and throughout the day helps me to stay in alignment with Spirit and "hear" God's Voice, which comes in so many different forms; in this case my own built-in GPS that guided me straight to where I needed to be.

My heart was already open to God's Love as I entered the store; such was my gratitude for the guidance I had just received. I browsed around for a while and eventually decided on a basketball hoop for toddlers that can be attached to a door or wall and used for indoor play. It was either between that or a freestanding one, of which there was only one left, and that one had a few more bells and whistles and was more for outdoor use. I felt good about the choice I had made, paid for it, and left the store. However, as I reached the parking lot I began to second-guess my decision, thinking about the freestanding hoop and how that might be better. My mind began weighing out the pros and cons until next thing I know I was headed back into the store to possibly exchange it. I went to the customer service desk still undecided about which toy to get but leaning toward an exchange.

As I reached the desk and began to speak to the employee about what I was thinking, a man and his wife approached and asked the same employee if a certain toy was in stock. The toy was a request from their son who had just sent them the specific brand and model number on their smartphone. To my amazement, it was the exact same freestanding basketball hoop I had just come back in to possibly purchase. Of all the toys in Toys "R" Us, this was the one they were seeking! The couple was pleasantly surprised when I was able to tell them that their item was indeed in stock, and in fact, the only one left. I was even able to escort them to the section where it was, and sure enough it was exactly what they were looking for. They thanked me and left with their purchase.

To me this was an obvious confirmation that my original instincts had been right. My mind had started to talk me out of what my heart already knew, but Divine Spirit intervened and gave me an "awake dream," an out of the ordinary experience that got my attention, through the couple who were looking for the same toy. Not only did this help me with my choice, but the other family got served as well. They were able to find the right toy for their son, even receiving personal customer service in the process. It was clearly a win-win situation!

As if that wasn't enough, and as the saying goes, "Now for the rest of the story." Later on I was telling my girlfriend about my Toys "R" Us adventure and she told me she and her son already had an outdoor freestanding basketball hoop. In fact, they had just taken it out of the garage the other day after a long winter and played in the early spring sunshine. She did not however, have one for indoors and said it would be perfect for inclement weather when he needed an outlet and couldn't play outside. So the indoor wall-unit was indeed the perfect gift! I did not know this at the time, but the one who guides me knows everything.

Some people speak of the grand miracles they may need to offer proof of God's existence, but to me the miracles are in the myriad everyday details of our lives that Spirit weaves itself into. To me that "weave" IS the miracle. God's Love was woven into every step I took that day, as it is every day. We are all inextricably linked and connected to that love if we only open our eyes to see it. God loves each of us personally, cares about what is important to us, and wants to bless us, from our greatest undertakings to the simplicity of finding a child's toy.

Written by Laurence Elder

31

Lesson From an Ancient Prophet

What sets a spiritual great apart from others? For one, a sense of selflessness. They serve all life out of a deep love with no thought of reward. In doing so, they are actually rewarded greatly; they gain life by serving life. The Love of God flows to them and through them showing itself in all they do.

In my bedroom hang the portraits of nine Prophets of Old. Divinely inspired teachers who, in their day, were ordained by God to speak for Him. These ancient teachers are still fully operational, able to teach us in dreams.

During this dream the portraits were hanging on my bedroom wall much like in the physical, but two of the Prophets' pictures hovered in midair in the middle of my bedroom, like a hologram. I thought I was awake and seeing an optical illusion. I took my glasses off to look again. The pictures were still there. I cleaned my glasses and put them back on. The pictures still hung in midair! That's when I realized, this is a spiritual experience! I gazed steadily into one of the floating holograms. It displayed the face of an African holy man from an ancient kingdom. As I gazed at his portrait, the following scene unfolded.

The face of this ancient teacher shifted before my eyes. In the picture he's portrayed with a distinguished white beard, but as I watched it transformed to a younger man's face. It was still him, but with the black beard of a man in his prime. He stood with his back to a wall, a servant in an ancient kingdom. Holding a tray of food, he wore a friendly expression. One of the members of court, dressed in fanciful feathers and expensive cloth, walked by and selected a bit of food from the tray he held. This Prophet of Old nodded happily at this aristocrat, who seemed to have no idea this household servant was actually a spiritual giant. A warm smile graced the Prophet's face; he was truly happy to serve in this most humble way.

The Prophet executed what many would consider a menial task with an open heart, full of joy and happiness. A simple act of serving food, and one that many people would do with a chip on their shoulder. This ancient wise man, one of the spiritual greats of history, regarded his humble task as a privilege. He saw the blessing of serving another Soul. We have heard many times that "Service is its own reward." Through this simple interaction, this great Soul demonstrated it without a single word. The Love of God flowed through him purely, bringing joy and blessings to this everyday interaction.

Through taking retreats at Guidance for a Better Life, I have learned that we too can open our hearts and allow God's Love to fill us and flow through us. Even the most mundane task becomes profound when motivated by love. The dream served as a bit of a wake-up call. Have I been going about my day with a chip on my shoulder? Have I been giving purely of myself, as this ancient Master did? I awoke with a new ideal; an image to carry of how I aspire to be in daily life. Remembering his smile and open heart reminds me of what service really is. With the help of the *current* Prophet of God, I strive to make this ideal a reality in my own life each day.

Written by David Hughes

32

A Stranger's Approach Was a Godsend

∽⁊∾

As a gift of love God can send someone into our life to remind us of what we hold most dear. This opportunity to more deeply appreciate the things in life we value is such a blessing. Especially when it is one of the most sacred things — the HU Song.

Did you ever have an interesting and out of the ordinary interaction with a stranger that left you asking yourself, "What was that all about?" One that has actually stayed with you many years afterward? One day in the year 2000 I had that happen.

I was in a grocery store I had shopped at many times. After shopping the produce department I was standing in the center of the aisle near the meat section when I felt someone looking at me. I looked up and noticed an elderly woman with white straight hair and blue eyes pushing a shopping cart. She was heavyset and dressed in what appeared to be a housedress. It was very clear she was coming toward me, and it also seemed the physical store and all the contents on the shelves along with the shelves themselves faded into the background, highlighting even more her approach.

When she arrived we stood facing one another, and then she asked if I had any money. I pulled out my wallet and looked inside and saw I had very little in my wallet that day, but I remembered I did have something. I had a HU card, the most precious gift ever given to me. HU is a prayer, a love song to God, and when sung purely it helps to tune us into the stream of God's unconditional Love. I instinctively reached in my wallet and handed the card to her. I explained what was written on the card, what HU means, and how precious HU is and has been for me personally in my life.

She accepted it, and before I realized what was happening, she bent over slightly taking my hand into her own and kissed the top of my hand as she thanked me. She said that HU is worth a lot more than coins. I certainly was taken aback, yet I realized she, as Soul, truly recognized and connected with the true, pure, and precious gift. When this amazing interaction was complete, the white-lit room reshaped itself into its original form as I viewed her walking away. Interestingly enough, I did not see her again throughout the store. I looked for her but she was gone.

And so I was blessed that day because God sent one of His helpers to remind me what was truly important: my own connection with HU, and the value I placed on it. Since that day HU has become even more valuable to me. I still today think of that lovely woman who helped open my eyes to better appreciate what was already true in my heart.

Written by Moira Cervone

33

Taking Care of Business

When facing challenges in life we can handle them
better if we surrender to the guidance and flow of Spirit.
Prophet can lead us through anything. This doesn't
mean we don't make the effort to prepare and plan; we
still need to do our part. The greatest of which is
being receptive to Divine guidance.

During some of the early years in which I
attended retreats at Guidance for a Better Life
my teacher mentioned enjoying the song "Takin'
Care of Business," by Bachman-Turner Overdrive,
and we even listened to it during some of our
breaks. Although I remembered this song from
when I was a teenager, it took on a whole new
dimension in light of the spiritual training I was
receiving. Not only is it fun, upbeat, and
motivating, it also reminds me of how we are
here to "take care of business" spiritually — to
wake up to our true Divine nature, nurture our
personal connection with God, and help others
to discover their divinity. Over time this song has

become part of my personal "awake dream" language. When I hear it, it opens my heart, reminds me of my spiritual priorities, and of my cherished relationship with my teacher Prophet Del Hall.

In the past year I have been blessed with a huge door opening in my life; after decades of being a freelance professional musician I am now teaching music at a college. It is both fun and exciting, yet extremely challenging. I find myself way out of my comfort zone much of the time, dancing on the precipice where preparation meets surrender. I have pondered on the fact, that some of the things I have been doing professionally for so many years are much more challenging to teach than I thought they might be.

Recently I sat in my car about fifteen minutes before my afternoon songwriting class began asking Prophet for help. Although I think I was doing a satisfactory and functional job delivering the material, there was a flow, or a "sweet spot" I just had not found yet. I was following a rigid outline and nervous to depart from it. I knew my students had way more potential than had been brought out, and so much more to share if they just felt a little more comfortable opening up. I knew there was more. I also knew there was nothing I could do to make that happen; I had to surrender. I sang HU for several minutes, helping me relax, let go of my mind chatter, and focused inwardly on spiritual guidance.

As I entered the classroom I felt a strong nudge from Prophet to put on the song "Takin' Care of Business." The guidance was just to put the song on, without introducing it or saying a word. After it was done playing, I began a discussion with the class. It turned out the song was a perfect segue into the outline I had already planned for the day. Instead of sticking to the outline however, I allowed the discussion to unfold in a much more spontaneous way. One by one the students shared on a deeper level than I had ever heard before, and I was talking less and listening more. I felt I was more in the role of a "facilitator," which is something I have witnessed and aspired to from observing my teachers Del and Del IV facilitate their retreats.

I am grateful for being given the experience of being a facilitator that day. By surrendering my personal agenda and going "off-script," I was actually more in alignment with God's script and in the flow of Spirit. And the prayer that was in my heart was answered: more important than covering my exact lesson plan that day was my desire that the students and I share an experience of openness and connection. The points in my outline that were important still got covered, but in a more seamless and inspired way than I could have ever planned or thought of on my own. God loves each of us and wants to help us take care of the everyday business of our lives, whatever that may be. Thank you Prophet for always knowing the best ways to help me "take care of business!"

Written by Laurence Elder

34

The Love You Always Wanted

The experience of meeting an aspect of God is profound and deeply personal; it fills you with God's Love and leaves you lacking nothing. The idea of partaking in a spiritual journey home to God might be hard for some to believe. It is, however, truly possible if you have a spiritual guide who is authorized to show you the way.

The experience of God is like nothing in this world. It can shatter your limitations, transform your heart, and change your life. It can give blessings far beyond what you ever thought to ask for. It can fill you with love; the love you had always hoped for, but never knew for sure was really out there. The experience of God can do all this and more. I have been blessed to see the Face of God many times. These Divine experiences were made possible by the guidance of the current living Prophet of God,

Del Hall III of Virginia. Years of Del's guidance led me to see God face-to-face. The following paragraphs describe one such experience and the Divine impact it has had on my life.

It was a clear Sunday morning at Guidance for a Better Life, and a group was gathered in the building we call the Beach House. The group took their seats and we prepared to sing HU, an ancient love song to God. Del led us in a sacred and beautiful opening prayer, and we began. The harmony of praiseful voices filled the room. Gently my awareness shifted from my physical body sitting in the Beach House to my spiritual side, Soul, the real me. As Soul I was aware of being on the shore of a vast ocean of love and mercy with Prophet. We knelt on the sand in reverence, then approached the sparkling, golden waters of God. As we entered the water God's Love permeated my very being. It was refreshing and nourishing. Peace and contentment filled me as I drank deeply. Then a tremendous white light appeared over the waves. It emanated the intense yet nurturing Love of God, for this was no ordinary light but an aspect of God Himself. With Prophet's help I opened myself to be as receptive as possible to this experience of God. Slowly, a face appeared in the light. A face that radiated the most profound love, wisdom, and power one could imagine. As the eyes fell upon me, it felt almost like I was melting into God's pure Love and truth.

Basking in God's mighty Presence, old misunderstandings of God, life, and truth crumbled away. More room was made in my heart for accepting love and truth. An extraordinary feeling of blessedness and gratitude flowed through me. What gift had I been given? Was it even possible to put into words? I knew this much — God's gaze gave me a greater capacity to love, to serve Him, and to accept truth.

Afterwards, as I sat contemplating what had just happened, I saw the Face of God again, but this time it was not directed at me. He was pouring His golden Light and Love all over our beautiful blue planet. I know His Love is gently marinating our planet, preparing, and nurturing Souls for a great upliftment that is to come.

I feel so blessed to have been given this glorious experience, and many like it. God's Love is the love so many seek, yet do not know where or how to find. It can be found through His current living Prophet. He can guide you home to God, as he has done for me and many others.

Written by David Hughes

35

Opening a Gift From God

God is actively reaching out to bless, guide, and comfort His children. Many people miss this because they have no reference for what these expressions of God's Love for us look like, or they too easily allow their minds to blow it off. A living teacher, one who knows the ways of Spirit and can help you understand your experiences, is imperative for those seeking to truly know God.

Imagine you found a forgotten, unopened gift tucked away in a closet. When you saw the gift was for you, your curiosity would likely become excitement. The love put into choosing and wrapping the gift would still be there, waiting to reach your heart. I recently found such a gift, and it was from God. While looking through my old journals, I found notes about my first three-day spiritual retreat at Guidance for a Better Life in 1997. I had a lot of fear then, especially of speaking in front of people, and though I longed to have spiritual experiences myself, I feared they might be too much and scare me. I did not see then how perfect my experiences were for me, chosen with loving care by God.

On the second night of that retreat, we gathered and sang a long HU. Though we sat very close together, I felt expansiveness around me, as if I were in a huge room. I opened my heart as much as I could and looked into the darkness, hoping to see something. With closed eyes, I saw a white light, like a star in the sky, and another light that turned before me like a small spotlight. I wondered if this was the Light of God Del had spoken of, or just the light I often saw at night. For years I would sometimes see light in various colors float across my vision in a dark room. I enjoyed watching them, but I never thought much about what they were beyond assuming it was a physical phenomenon.

The next day I listened as other students shared their experiences. Often they began by saying they really had not experienced anything. No matter how amazing the experience, doubt can creep in, especially if the experience is new and not understood. As they shared, Del helped one student after another recognize that what they experienced was a gift from God. Some felt peace, some felt love, and some saw the Light of

God. As the weekend progressed, I stopped being surprised to hear how unexpectedly blessed each Soul was. Still, I doubted my own experiences. It is much easier to see how loved another Soul is, how blessed they are. This can be a first step, recognizing a gift or quality in someone else, and then eventually seeing it in oneself.

Realizing God's Love was truly for me too took longer. I let fear stop me from sharing my experience that weekend. What might I have learned then if I had shared, gaining help and wisdom from Prophet? In my memories I found the gift still there, waiting to be opened. When sharing His Love, God does not want to scare His children. He showed me His Light, which is love, in a gentle way that was already familiar to me. Not only was I just as blessed as my fellow students, I had been for years. Every time I saw light in a dark room, what I thought was some physical thing in my eyes, was really God saying "I love you." This realization rippled through my memories like a healing. Knowingness of God's Love and blessings replaced how I felt and thought of myself then. By seeing the truth, I gained a new perspective that shifted how I saw that moment and all that came after.

Would my life be different now had I found the courage to share then, if I had understood then how blessed I was? I will never know what might have been. I savor this blessing now and wonder what other treasures lay in my journals and memories, waiting to be opened. What treasures lie within your memories or heart? Is there a dream so special you have never forgotten it? Was there a coincidence that seemed far beyond what chance could bring? These gifts still wait to be opened. Within lies this truth — you too are loved and blessed by God.

Written by Jean Enzbrenner

36

Another Moment Together

Many have longed for another moment with a loved
one who has passed on. They look forward to the day
when they are reunited in Heaven. Please know you can
visit with your loved ones now in dreams and spiritual
contemplations. These experiences are just as
real; do not discount them.

On a beautiful summer morning during a
weeklong retreat at Guidance for a Better Life I
was given a very short dream. During it my
spiritual teacher, Del Hall, asked me, "Did you
get to see your dad?" He was referring to the
experiences we had during a HU Sing at the
retreat the night before. At that very moment I
remembered seeing a glimpse of my dad
towards the very end of the HU Sing that I had
forgotten. I wrote it in my journal and thanked
Prophet for this gift of remembrance.

Later that morning as I closed my eyes in appreciation, I wished my dad well. I knew Prophet's presence was with me, and I could feel his love in a warm breeze. As I did my dad spiritually appeared right in front of me! I hugged him and felt his bony shoulder as I leaned my head on it. I miss him so much. My eyes watered as they are watering now, reliving this gift. Wow! I got to spend a few moments with my dad who passed away a few years back. God gave me this tailor-made experience through His chosen Prophet. Prophet loves me and knows me so well. You too can be blessed with such precious moments.

Written by Olga Boucher

37

God's Love is All Around Us

We are here on Earth to learn more about giving and receiving love. Of the two, more tend to struggle with receiving love rather than giving love. Fortunately, the Divine presents us with countless opportunities to practice, for if one desires to truly give love they must first be able to receive it. We cannot pass on what we do not have.

I attended a wonderful reunion recently. There I was blessed to experience God's Love in a circumstance that was different than I would have imagined. Every moment can be an opportunity to give or receive love, no matter where we are — at church or at home, at work or at the store, or as in this example — cutting cheesecake.

It was a perfect mid-summer evening. I was standing around the table with my family and friends, enjoying the sweet laughter and familiar sounds of those I love while I was slicing cheesecake for dessert. Suddenly, I began to feel weak and I fainted. Two men standing at the table beside me caught me as I began to fall. My husband watched me begin to faint and raced around the table to catch me before I hit the ground.

For those of you who have fainted before, you can probably relate to the anxiety when you come back into your body, unaware as to why people are looking down at you with such concern. Slowly I realized what had happened. With my husband at my side like a rock of solid love, I received a chair in which to rest until I gained back my strength. A friend who is a physician's assistant began to ask me questions to decipher what had happened, but there seemed to be no logical explanation for it. It was an unexpected and random event which contained a hidden blessing.

As I was recovering in the chair, I became aware that God was opening a window for me. Through it He was revealing a greater portion of His Love for me through my friends and family. I knew at that moment He has that same love for each and every one of us, including you. More love than we could possibly imagine is all around us — *all the time.*

For the next ten minutes as I regained stability, I could feel God's Love pouring into me. I could now see what had always been there. Gratitude streamed out of my heart. I am so blessed to love and be loved by my husband. His strength and devotion became even more apparent to me that night, shining forth through a turbulent moment. How sweet that was and still is!

Around the room stood other people in my life whom I love and who love me. Disguised as human love, I received a portion of God's Love in each thought or prayer of well wishes and each compassionate look in their eyes. As a friend handed me a glass of water, it was God's Love that was passed into my hand and heart. Each touch on the shoulder, each cold rag on my forehead, did the same. They were all gifts of love from God, just in different forms – given from Soul to Soul. It was a very precious moment. To be loved is no little thing, but a huge gift from God that I cherish.

I also felt so protected. I had been in precarious places to faint earlier that day — at the edge of a creek, on a large rock in the woods, and alone in the bathroom. Yet I fainted at the precise moment in time where I could receive the most care. I could see the concern in my husband's and friends' eyes, understandably, but I knew that somehow this was part of God's plan for me. Throughout the whole experience, I was blessed to be keenly aware of the presence of God's Prophet with me. His presence gives me comfort and security that transcend any physical experience. With him I was aware of a sphere of soft golden and white light surrounding me and the entire room. Inwardly, Prophet gave me reassurance that everything was fine, which helped me to relax and be present in the moment.

On this wonderful summer evening, I was given the opportunity to see and accept more of God's Love. For years Del Hall has taught me and others to recognize God's Hand and His Love in all areas of our lives. And in this moment of physical vulnerability, God's message got through to me. I saw His Love in everything and everyone around me. Throughout my life, I like many others, have found it easier to give love than to receive it. This night was an opportunity to just accept it. Thank you Prophet for helping me to see and accept more of what has always been around me – *God's Love.*

Written by Molly Comfort

38

Thank You Letter to God

It is not enough to simply have love for another; love must be expressed in order for it to make a difference. This applies to the love we have for others in our lives and for our love of God. Yes our love is known, but expressing it is the greatest blessing for everyone involved.

In a relationship, the ability to give and receive love with your beloved is a very special and important component. Knowing your loved one heard, felt, and accepted your expression of love for them is truly a gift. I have so much love and gratitude for God in my heart, and while I trust that He knows, I cherish every opportunity to express it to Him. During one retreat Prophet offered us the sacred opportunity to write a thank you card to God in our hearts, and then deliver it to Him.

"Dearest Beloved God, Words cannot express my love and gratitude. Please read my heart. I

love you so much. Thank you for everything. My existence. My eternity. Every fiber/all of me as light and sound thanks you. I have never been happier both physically and spiritually. Thank you for my spiritual journey and allowing me to serve other Souls in your mission. I hope you know how much you are in my thoughts and heart daily. I love you — Soul"

Then we continued to sing HU, and I felt like my letter continued to be written and conveyed from my heart. Words were not added, but while singing HU, a love song to God, the gratitude and love from the letter kept flowing to God. My heart burst with love for my creator. Then Prophet, continuing to guide us in contemplation, escorted us into the Heavens and to the primary Abode of God to personally deliver our letters to an aspect of God.

We arrived at an ocean full of love and mercy, God's primary abode. As Soul I stood on a beach of golden sand and gazed in awe out over an expansive ocean of light. On the horizon I saw a beautiful mansion appear. The mansion reminded me of the Bible verse, "In my Father's house are many mansions: if it were not so, I would have told you. I go to prepare a place for you." John 14:2 KJV I delivered the letter inside the mansion, which was an expanse of all white light and electrified with sound. I felt nourished, safe, secure, and loved, and like I had finally come home.

Then, in an interesting twist, I heard what sounded like thousands of geese flying overhead. I knew immediately in my heart that God had received my letter! I love the physical sound of geese and now, as above so below, I will remember delivering my letter to God whenever I hear geese overhead during my daily life. Remembrance of that sacred moment brings Heaven to Earth, and I am filled with the same love and peace as I felt when I delivered my love letter to God. Thank you Prophet for giving me the opportunity to express even a portion of my love for God directly to Him, and to know I was heard and am loved in return.

Written by Catherine Hughes

39

One Door Closes Another Opens

Each of us is Soul, a Divine child of God that can be used by Spirit as a blessing to others. To allow the "Word" to flow through us it is best to be "tuned in." Singing God's Holy name, HU, with love in our hearts is one of the best ways to do this. There is no greater joy than allowing the Holy Spirit to work through us to bless another.

After I received a job transfer I met one of my new coworkers, Sandy. Within my first week I found out Sandy was quitting her job at the end of the week because management would not let her change her schedule so she could pick up her daughter from school. She was very helpful getting me acclimated to my new surroundings, and I was a little bummed out she was leaving. On Friday several employees planned a party for Sandy to wish her well in the new life she was about to embark on. Friday morning before work I tuned in to the Divine by singing HU, a love song to God, and also declared myself a clear channel so I could be ready to assist Prophet in sending God's Love to wherever it's needed. Little did I know God had a special blessing for Sandy. I was about to be called into service as a coworker with Prophet to help pass on his blessings.

About nine o'clock all the employees were called over to the banquet tables that were set up with lots of food and drink in honor of Sandy's last day at work. As I made my way over to get some food I found my feet wanted to go in a different direction. Sandy was a couple tables away from me, and I soon realized I was being pulled toward her as if by a "tractor beam" from science fiction movies. It became clearer as I got closer to Sandy, because Divine Spirit was downloading words into my heart to share with her. While she was getting something to drink I stepped up next to her and said, "It takes a lot of guts to do what you are doing and most people wouldn't quit their job." The next thing Divine Spirit gave me to say was, "This is kind of how the Holy Spirit works, you close one door and another door opens, so don't worry, everything is going to work out." Sandy looked at me with her eyes about as wide open as they could get, which told me she knew the words I had just spoken were not from me but from God.

Only God could know what she needed at that moment as she was about to give up her livelihood.

Now for the rest of the story. Shortly after she left, Sandy was hired at a similar position in a different office where they had no problem working with her schedule. Sandy's story can teach us to trust in God and His current Prophet, who can help us navigate through life's changes even if we are not aware of his presence. Del, my spiritual teacher at Guidance for a Better Life, is God's Prophet of the times who is here to help all Souls, and has personally helped me through many of my life's changes.

If you desire to be more aware of how the Divine works in your life, sing HU several times throughout the day to tune in to the Divine. As your awareness of the Divine Hand of God increases, so will your joy in life. Especially when going through uncertain times like Sandy, you will know God has got your back. This happy ending brings to mind the Bible scripture: "Behold the fowls of the air: for they sow not, neither do they reap, nor gather into barns; yet your heavenly Father feedeth them. Are ye not much better than they?" Matthew 6:26 KJV

Written by Sam Spitale

40

The Process of Freeing Me

*Prophet leads his students through the process of
awakening to their true eternal selves, Soul. This is
done through experiences in both the waking and
sleeping states. He gently peels back the layers of
untruth and removes blocks to God's Love, truth, and
ways. The result — an abundant life.*

My inner and outer relationship with God's
true Prophet has been the key to unlocking what
has held me back, perhaps for lifetimes, from
real freedom, joy, deep peace, security, balance,
and knowing God loves me, personally, as He
loves each of us, personally. One of the first
retreats I took at Guidance for a Better Life was
on wilderness skills. Though we were engaged in
much physical work, Del Hall began to teach to
all who would listen, profound lessons as the
Divine came through him. He did not force
teachings on us; it is his nature to see the
blessings in all life and he shares what comes
through him freely. He suggested we pay

attention to dreams while we were at the retreat. He had found many of his students were able to remember some interesting dreams while on the property that helped them in their lives. If we wanted to we could ask for dreams that night.

My dreams were usually long and seemed senseless, but I asked for a dream that night because there was something about Del. Everything he said, and even when he did not say anything, was genuine, truthful, and motivated by love of truth. I listened to him, and he quenched a thirst I did not know I had. My thirst was not related to the physical labor of practicing wilderness skills. It was Soul's thirst for its freedom and for God's truth.

I was given two short dreams that very night. In one, Del was holding me up in the air. We hovered over a dumpster, a big orange dumpster. Orange is a predominant color of the Causal plane of God's Worlds, where karmic patterns from lifetimes are stored along with other past-life records. Del put things in that dumpster for me, things I did not need. I asked if I could help. He said no, not yet. He said there were three locks that he knew how to undo to put things in the dumpster, and I did not know how to open those locks yet. Through that dream I was allowed to see God's own true Prophet, Del Hall, in one of the roles he fulfills from God, that of Redeemer. The Redeemer, as a vehicle for God, can lift individuals closer to spiritual liberation.

In the other dream my boss from many years ago, a librarian, was in a birdcage, with the door closed. It was actually the "little self" side of me in that cage, not the librarian. The Dream Master, another role or aspect of the Prophet, blessed me with this truth about myself. However, my subconscious mind, trying to protect me, toned it down by censoring it through the symbols of the librarian in the birdcage – so as not to alarm me. I was not free to live as my real self, Soul, yet. God sends the Prophet, as Redeemer, to help Soul help itself be free.

God endows each of us with a truth detector, which is a vital attribute of Soul. My truth detector recognized the Voice of God coming through Del, and I would return to the retreat center for more living waters to quench my spiritual thirst. I began to learn of spiritual keys that could unlock my heart and begin the process of freeing me of worry, fear, vanity, guilt, lack of confidence; the whole slew of the human consciousness experience that was wearing me down and tearing me up. Del taught HU, which is a love song to God, a prayer to God. HU is sung directly to God. Soul begins to awaken and be tuned to God's channel, instead of the channel of the mind. HU, sung on a fairly regular basis, was one of the first keys to unlock my heart so Divine attributes like love, peace, trust, balance, and joy could flourish and begin to edge out the things I did not need anymore.

Del encouraged us to think of something we were really grateful for before we begin to sing HU. Gratitude is another key that opened my heart more. Thinking of one thing I was grateful for led to another, and another, and another. A more open heart is more receptive to Divine guidance. Prophet can place so many blessings from God in a grateful heart, such as love, clarity, peace, joy, and more.

HU and gratitude prepared, conditioned, and purified me enough so I could consciously meet with Prophet, be taught by him on the outer and inner, and develop a growing relationship of trust and love. This relationship is the jackpot key! Over time and with focus, these keys become a way of life. I continue to appreciate them even more: HU, gratitude, and my relationship with Prophet.

When I followed Del's suggestion and asked for a dream at that early retreat at Guidance for a Better Life, in effect letting the Divine know I was interested, I began a process of becoming a more active participant with the Hand of God in my life. Not just one area of my life would be improved, but all areas. With the help of Prophet and with deeper appreciation, I look back and see I have always been in the Hand of God throughout my life. So have you. I continue to ask for dreams and am so grateful for them, for they reach me, teach me, and are reflections of Soul's life in the planes of God's Worlds. Each of us has our own personal, individualized syllabus from God. How sweet it is to become more conscious of the love and freedom God has in store for you!

Written by Martha Stinson

41

Heaven on Earth

We live in this world but are not of it. We are so much more than our physical bodies; we are Soul, made from the Holy Spirit — the Light and Sound of God. Experiencing this true reality is a special blessing and opportunity available for Prophet's disciples.

I stood on the steps of God's Temple with Prophet as the other Souls in our group arrived. We had been invited here to visit this sacred temple and its guardian met us at the doorway. We traveled here in our Soul bodies, our true inner selves, safely escorted by Prophet. This was a rare opportunity we had been given to have individualized learning experiences that would nourish, cleanse, fortify us, and aid us in our spiritual growth.

The Prophet, the temple guardian, and I walked inside and without a word being exchanged went directly to the beam of God's Light and Sound in the center of the room. I could hear crackling and popping sounds of the dynamic life-giving energy of the beam; Its sound was loud in my ears. It did not appear as a solid beam of light as I had seen before, but as large white shimmering sheets of light that had texture. We went into It, and the three of us stood inside this beam of Light and Sound of God in our Soul bodies, which were also made of this same light and sound. Inside there was stillness and timelessness. The only word that could describe what I felt was "complete." I was complete. In this beam there was nothing I lacked. As Soul everything I could ever want or need was right there.

Just then, I became aware of being both inside the beam in the temple and also sitting in my chair back in the classroom. A long shaft of white light from the beam connected me in my Soul body inside the temple with me in my physical body that sat in the chair, the light coming straight into my heart. It felt as if a solid connection of God's Light and Love was made between these two aspects of me. I felt something was being downloaded through this light and was integrating into my physical being. There came a sense of continuity, oneness, and sameness between the part of me still in Heaven, the part of me on Earth, and the light that connected us. A shower of golden light then cleansed and nourished me. I asked for whatever might be holding me back in life to be let go. I cupped my hands and drank of this golden "water of love" as it poured over me and bathed me. I was so filled with love and appreciation for these gifts from Prophet that I spiritually danced in joy.

Soul as created by God is complete, but we are not always conscious of it down here in the physical. Often we search for things outside of us to make us feel whole, secure, or good enough. We forget our true nature, which is one reason God sends His Prophets. Prophet Del Hall helped me to remember who I really am, Soul. I have been his student for a long time. It has been a continuing process during which he has lovingly helped me recognize and manifest my own Divine qualities as Soul and come to know the real me. Through many experiences such as this one, he has helped the dormant qualities of Soul become activated. Prophet's inner form is the Light and Sound of God, the Holy Spirit, the Presence of the Divine. Experiencing myself as light and sound, Soul, in the beam at the temple was wonderful, but it was not that alone which brought about the feeling of completeness. It was being inside of Prophet's inner form as the

Light and Sound of God (the beam) that made it so; with him and in him I lack nothing.

The completeness I experienced inside the beam, feeling I had everything I could ever want or need, does not mean I now shun earthly comforts and pleasures or no longer welcome the blessings of family, friends, or material wealth. It just means I do not *need* those things to make me feel whole. It is so freeing to know I do not need material things for self-esteem or self-worth, nor do I need others to make me feel good about myself, looking to them to fill something I feel is lacking in me. I am free to express and accept love more purely, appreciating my loved ones and those I interact with for who they are and the joy they bring to my life with no strings attached.

These gifts from Prophet have added so much abundance, fulfillment, freedom, and sweetness to my life! I nurture them by staying spiritually close to him and by being present in his presence throughout the day. Living life in his presence is very much like living inside the beam of light and sound. It is the relationship with Prophet that brings the glories of Heaven into everyday reality while one is still living on this Earth.   Written by Lorraine Fortier

42
Rush Hour Emergency

Those with the eyes to see will see God's Love and blessings everywhere. Everything from the gift of life itself, right down to a series of green lights and a parking space when it's truly needed.

My dad was a double organ transplant recipient. His first transplant was a kidney. The second transplant was another kidney and a pancreas. The third transplant procedure was another kidney to replace the damaged one. The first kidney was damaged from the donor's accident. My family is well versed in praying, our belief in God, and miracles. We know how precious life is and are very grateful for each transplant. Our hearts also hurt, for there was a family somewhere mourning the loss of a loved one.

I was on a job site working ten-hour shifts when I received a phone call from my mom. "Your dad is going in for emergency surgery.

The doctor thinks his body is rejecting the kidney. Can you leave work and get to the hospital now? He is going in soon!" "Mom, I will be there." I immediately sang HU, an ancient love song to God, and asked God "Please, please get me to the hospital before he goes into surgery." I parked the machine I was operating and found the superintendent to inform him of what was going on. My job site was less than five miles from the hospital. When looking at my watch I realized it was the five o'clock rush hour, and everyone was heading home from work. "God, please get me to the hospital in time." I got into my vehicle and headed for the hospital. Every light was green except for one and even though it was rush hour, surprisingly, there was very little traffic. When I arrived there was a parking space close to the hospital entrance. With God's Grace and help, I made it to see and talk with my dad before the surgical team took him in for his operation.

While he was in surgery I prayed for God to be with the surgical team and for Thy will to be done. As I sat in the hallway, I had the realization of how many other people were in this hospital and surrounding hospitals there in the Pittsburgh, Pennsylvania area. How many people have loved ones they are concerned about and praying for? I prayed, "God, please bring comfort and peace to these people. Thank you for all that you do for us." I again sang HU as a thank you to God.

Several hours later the surgeon came out and informed us the kidney and pancreas were fine. A vein to the kidney had torn and was allowing toxins to leak into the body cavity. My dad's transplanted organs were not being rejected by his body. A miracle. Thank you Prophet and God for being there and taking care of everyone. Thank you for your blessings; getting me to the hospital on time, the miracle, and the precious gift of life.

Written by Rebecca Vettorel

43

My Spiritual Pantry

Just as your physical body needs physical food, your true spiritual self, Soul, needs spiritual food. Without daily spiritual nourishment you will wither. Yes, you may be alive, but this does not mean you truly have life.

It was the Sunday after Christmas 2015; I was drinking a delicious cup of coffee and just enjoying a day off from work. After doing some household chores I noticed I was very hungry. I was looking for something to eat and couldn't find anything until I looked in my fridge. There I found leftovers from Christmas dinner at my daughter's house that my son-in-law so kindly packed up for me to take home. I had forgotten they were there and quickly proceeded to fry up some of the ham to make the most awesome ham and egg "Dagwood" sandwich. Barely getting my mouth around the huge sandwich, I thought of how useless my food pantry is if the food is forgotten and not used. I could starve while having a fully stocked pantry of unused food.

This immediately reminded me of a major spiritual lesson I learned from Del, my spiritual teacher at Guidance for a Better Life. Del talked about our spiritual pantry, comparing it to a food pantry. A spiritual pantry is full of spiritual tools available to use to stay spiritually nourished. Tools such as singing HU, a love song to God, reading of scriptures, our journals full of recorded dreams and retreat experiences, and more to be used for our daily "spiritual bread." Soul needs nourishment just as the physical body needs food. As I was enjoying my sandwich I began to remember all the food dreams I have been given by Prophet to show me how I had been starving spiritually. That is when I made the connection about forgetting the food in the fridge, my food pantry, and how it parallels my lesson about my spiritual pantry. Using the tools in my spiritual pantry daily uplifts and raises the bar for all my physical life experiences. The main reason for this is that staying spiritually nourished helps us recognize God's blessings in our life and the presence of Prophet who is always with us.

Jesus said it much better in the Bible after he had been fasting in the wilderness for forty days and forty nights: "And when the tempter came to him, he said, If thou be the Son of God, command that these stones be made bread. But he answered and said, It is written, Man shall not live by bread alone, but by every word that proceedeth out of the mouth of God." Matthew 4:3-4 KJV This quote from the Bible shows us just how important spiritual nourishment is for us. If we stay nourished spiritually we can begin to enjoy the abundant life we were meant to live.

Written by Sam Spitale

44

Dream With Past-Life Records

It is true that you only live one life, but not in the sense that most people have been taught. You are Soul, an eternal spiritual being. You do not "have" a soul, you are Soul. You are one Soul, the same Soul, for all eternity. However, Soul lives many different physical lifetimes. Each serves as a unique opportunity to grow in wisdom and love.

During a morning contemplation I asked the Prophet for some insight about a relationship in my life. Afterwards I went about my day. Just before bed I thought about the things and people in my life that I am very grateful for. Then I drifted off to sleep.

I joined Prophet in a dream. We walked through a beautiful garden courtyard, entered a set of glass doors, and walked down a hallway into a very plain and simple room. After we sat and talked for a little while some people came in to visit with me. Most of the people I knew from the past, some of them were very good friends. A few of them I had not seen in years and others looked familiar but I could not recall from where. This caught my attention and raised some questions. Where was I and what was going on? Was it my birthday or had I died?

Prophet brought me back from my thoughts. He directed my attention from the people in the room to a nearby wall, which had a very beautiful and unusual wallpaper on it. It was made up of hundreds or thousands of tiny photos, images, or scenes. At a glance this made up a bigger picture. I was surprised when I noticed that the larger picture was an image of me. As a visual reference for the reader, a few weeks after this dream I came across an image made in a very similar way called a "Photo Mosaic." The image in my dream appeared to be alive and fluid. Though the majority of the images were unfamiliar, as I looked more closely I saw that a few of them were from significant periods in my present life.

Prophet explained to me that this giant collage was a record of many of my past lives. Hundreds and thousands of little images and scenes from hundreds and thousands of years.

As he talked he slowly walked down the hall, I followed. He turned, stopped, and faced the wall. There I noticed a small image that for some reason brought a smile to my face. In this picture there was an eighth century Chinese warrior who was riding a beautiful gray horse across rolling green hills. I knew it was me from a long time ago. I remembered that day, my horse, and that particular valley. In the picture next to it I saw myself walking in the hot desert during the time period when various pyramids were being built.

As I looked around I saw many other scenes and though the person I saw in them did not look the way I do now, I clearly knew that each had been me. The settings or surroundings I saw myself in varied widely. At times I had been in ancient forests or on white sandy beaches, inside castles, or next to primitive huts. And in other pictures I was in what appeared to be long forgotten cities or among civilizations that no longer existed.

The Prophet chuckled, and I looked over to see what he was looking at. "Here I am," he said pointing to a person in one of the scenes. "What were you doing?" I asked. He said, "Watching you, cheering you on!" He smiled. As he did he gazed into my eyes and I felt an incredible wave of love wash through me. I remembered this ancient love from many other lives deep in my heart. He showed me many such lifetimes, picture after picture where he, the Prophet, was watching over me, guiding me, and indeed cheering me on. In most of the lifetimes I had not been aware of the Prophet's presence, though in some of them I was blessed to be aware of and to have a conscious relationship with him.

When I looked back at the pictures again, many of the images were moving and playing out a scene from a specific time. The Prophet took his hand and touched one of the pictures. As he did it zoomed forward and the picture became life sized and alive. We walked inside this living scene. For that moment, while I was in the scene, I had no recall of being in the hallway looking at pictures or of sleeping in my warm bed. I was fully immersed in the experience of that life. I could see, smell, feel, and experience every detail of that time period as clearly as if I was living in it in the present moment. When I had remembered that life, the lesson, and the love, we stepped back out into the hallway with a smooth, flawless transition. I looked at many different images. The Prophet offered to take me and we went back into any of the lives that I was drawn to or had questions about. This trip back through my personal ancient history was incredible and "off the chart" amazing!

I came back with a new sense of peace and appreciation for the lives we live and how our relationships with others spans across eons from one time period to the next. Though our bodies may change in appearance, the relationships and/or strong bonds of love we form continue on with us from one life to another. I saw many people I knew then and could identify as the same Soul now, even though they looked different physically. In some of the lives I was a white person, in some a black person, in some Chinese, in some male and in some female. The color, sex, or nationality I had been seemed trivial and irrelevant in the big picture. The variations and combinations of race, gender, and nationality are endless but each life is specifically designed to help us experience and learn from a new perspective.

I saw that in different lifetimes I would reincarnate with many of the same Souls. Sometimes we had good relationships and sometimes we rubbed each other like course sandpaper, but each life had a common thread, which was to teach us all how to give and receive love. Sometimes we were friends, sometimes not, sometimes work associates, other times warriors in combat, the list was endless; farm workers, family members, children or parents, husbands or wives. I thank the Prophet for this incredible gift. It provided me with a much clearer understanding of how we are connected, and it helped me to have a greater love and appreciation for all the unique Souls and relationships I am blessed by God to have in my life. Through this dream gift, the Prophet also allowed me to see how each person and each life encouraged growth in many different areas. I awoke back in my warm bed.

Later I found out that the Prophet had taken me to the Causal Plane to a Temple of Golden Wisdom called Sakapori located in the spiritual city of Honu and the images and lifetimes I saw were kept in what is known as the Akashic records. We had been invited into this particular temple by Shamus-i-Tabriz, the Guardian of the Temple and keeper of these records.

The way that the Prophet can show us our past lives is as varied and individual as each person. I have seen some of my past lives as files in a file cabinet, been shown them in dreams, in contemplations, in the beam of light at a Spiritual Temple, and had glimpses or flashes of them in the course of a normal day. One of the main reasons to be shown past lives is to help us live a better, more fulfilling, joyful, and abundant life this time. Another reason is to help us realize that we are Soul, an eternal spark of God and that the real us does not die when our current bodies wear out. A third, and perhaps the most important reason, is to help us know that each Soul, whether consciously aware of it or not has had a long and personal relationship with God and It's Prophets through many lifetimes. When we come to the point in our lifetimes that we are able to consciously recognize God's Love for us and then our love for God, we and our lives become greatly blessed.

From this dream and other experiences I have realized that past lives are as real as any day in this present life. We have good days and tough days, but we each do the best we can. Each day, like each life, we live, love, grow, and learn a little more. It takes thousands of days in thousands of lifetimes to experience and learn about all the wonderful things that God has in store for us and to receive all the gifts and blessings that God wants to give us. We exist because God loves us. The lives in which we grow the most are the ones in which we are blessed to have a conscious relationship with and learn from a true Prophet of God. Our potential rate of growth in these lifetimes is exponential. With the Prophet's help, guidance, and love we can see the world and God more clearly as It truly is and come to know our Heavenly Father more intimately. This provides a life that is abundant beyond imagination.

Whether we are aware of it or not, God and His Prophet are always with us, seen or unseen, guiding, loving, nudging, rooting for and cheering us on during our journey home to our Heavenly Father.

Written by Jason Levinson

45

In the Care of the Lord

Many times when God answers a prayer it is written off as merely coincidence. This is unfortunate because one of the greatest blessings in life is actually being aware of your blessings. God does not need the credit; it is we who benefit. When we recognize and are grateful for the gifts of God's Love in our life it opens our heart to even more love.

God has blessed me with a daughter. Being her mom is the most wondrous privilege! I am in awe watching her grow and discover new things. Since she was born I have delighted in finding new ways for her to explore. One thing she loves to do is touch our cat Lila's fur. If left to her own devices she would get two fistfuls and a mouthful of cat hair. Lila will have none of this of course, and so I began to seek out other soft things for my daughter to play with instead.

I originally wanted to get her an animal pelt, but I could not find one. Then I found that sheepskins were sold online. The website showed babies rolling around snuggling with the fur. I thought my daughter would love this! However, the cost was more than I was willing to pay. Over time I would find myself once again looking at the sheepskins and then realizing it was not something she truly needed, and I would abandon the idea. One afternoon my husband, daughter, and I went for a walk down the street. Our neighbor Jeff was having a yard sale and we really enjoy talking with him so we stopped to visit. On our way out to continue the walk, something from the sale caught my eye. It was a large sheepskin rug! It was one of the exact brands I was looking at online. I took it to Jeff and asked how much it was. He insisted I take the rug as a gift. I was so excited because I knew this was a gift from God!

One of the special facets of being with Prophet is seeing the deeper meaning behind life's events that seem like coincidences. Prophet spoke to my heart, saying that if he would provide even this for my daughter, then he was absolutely providing everything else she needed. My daughter loves the sheepskin. She sits on it while she plays every day. When I see it I have a beautiful reminder of God's Love and protection for my daughter. In all circumstances she is in the care of the Lord.

Written by Carmen Snodgrass

46

HU – An Ancient Name of God

When you express your love and gratitude to God by singing HU, it is received; you are most certainly heard. Deeper realizations and insights on the profound blessing of HU will continue to grow every year for those who sing it.

Each spring the students of Guidance for a Better Life and their families come together for a Spring Clean-up Weekend to help prepare the retreat center for the coming year. On the surface it looks like work, but really it is sheer joy. Traditionally the weekend includes a bountiful potluck dinner Saturday evening and a family HU Sing Sunday morning.

This year we gathered in the Beach House on Sunday morning as in years past. My view from where I was seated at the back of the room allowed me to see all the families together and the excitement and smiles of the children. I love hearing their beautiful voices and it is a treat having them join us. Prophet Del Hall began by reviewing and explaining that HU is both a love song to God and an ancient name for God, and when we sing it we are essentially calling His name. He reminded us to be fully present in the moment when singing HU, to put love into how we sing, paying attention to how we form the word and enunciate the sound, and to do our best to sing in a pleasant, natural tone that blends harmoniously with others. In this way we demonstrate love and reverence to God.

Prophet then did something I will never forget to emphasize the profound sacredness of singing HU. He did a kind of role-play, acting out what it might be like as God hears us calling to Him by singing His name. In a light-hearted but purposeful way, he turned away from us and pretended to be God busy at whatever He might be doing. When God hears someone singing His name and calling to Him he turns to them and asks, "Yes my child, what can I do for you?" Prophet turned and looked directly at us as he said these words, but he was no longer play-acting; it was real. Physically I was in the last row of a room full of people when he did this, but my inner experience was as if I was the only one in the room. I was up very close to him, face to face, and God was looking right at me through the eyes of Prophet. In His eyes was eternity. An endless well of Divine love poured out, seared through me, knew me, and melted my heart. Love poured out of me back to Him. In an instant I was nurtured, loved, comforted, reassured, strengthened, and personally recognized by Almighty God, my Heavenly Father. My heart was so full, and I felt more tender and softened as I sang this beautiful love song and ancient name of God, carefully forming and savoring every precious HU I sang to Him.

This experience has sweetened and renewed every HU since. I remember how it felt to be held in that gaze of Divine love. I re-experience how that love tenderized my heart and brought forth an even greater love and appreciation to express back. Singing HU was an incredibly beautiful prayer before this, and now it is even more beautiful, more personal, and more sacred. I feel closer to my Heavenly Father, and though I know He hears every HU, every prayer, somehow this experience has made this knowing exist at an even deeper level and be even more real. Prophet taught me about HU over twenty years ago. In the time since he has revealed some of Its profound blessings and has given layer upon layer of experiences, understanding, and insights, and yet there is still more to learn, as I experienced here.

What happened this day also shows that, as a Prophet of God, Del can be teaching in a room full of people and be working with each one of his students individually on a very personal level. It gives one a glimpse into the Divine nature of Prophet and one of his many aspects, the Voice of God. He also provides a perfectly clear channel for God to reach out to us. What I experienced is really what Prophet's mission is all about: to take down walls and remove barriers between God and His children, to strengthen our communication and love connection with God, and to bring us closer together with our Father in Heaven.

Written by Lorraine Fortier

47

Be Still and Know

*Heaven is real, and those who have been blessed to
make the journey while still living know it cannot be
done alone. Fortunately God always has a Prophet on
Earth who knows the way and is authorized to return
Soul home to God to experience God's
Love and Grace.*

During a HU Sing at a spiritual retreat in the
summer of 2015 I was taken by Prophet and
blessed with this incredible experience with God.
In class I sat quietly with Prophet, as I did, I felt a
sense of peace, comfort, and love envelope me.
Together we sang HU. I was then consciously
taken through time and space to where they,
time and space, no longer exist.

I was now aware of being immersed in the
most magnificent Divine light. This light
nourished, fortified, cleansed, and purified me
through and through. I experienced an
overwhelming sense of gratitude and reverence

and dropped to my knees. Already on his knees next to me was Prophet, my inner teacher and guide, the Wayshower who is also the way. He is the one who has lovingly guided me through hundreds of lifetimes and brought me to this moment. Again my awareness was flooded with a brilliant white light, and I was being bathed in the gentle living waters of the Divine. As my eyes adjusted I found myself before a set of beautifully illuminated steps. I could barely look up towards the top; the light was so intense and almost overwhelming.

I knew where I was because by the Grace of God, Prophet had brought me here before. As I acclimated, I slowly raised my head and looked up. Before us sat God in all His magnificence, splendor, and glory! We were in our true home at the twelfth Heaven, the Abode of God. I was filled with a saturating peace, love, mercy, comfort, and joy. This place radiated with the brilliant Light of God and sweet heavenly music beyond description. God spoke directly to me as His Divine child. His Voice lovingly radiated through the Heavens and touched me to the core, "Be still and know I am God. I have loved you from the beginning, I love you now, and I will always love you. Please, accept my love." I allowed this Divine gift to wash through me.

Prophet invited me to stand up. We stood before our Heavenly Father, surrendering and yielding everything, totally open and receptive before Him. I felt God gently touch me and directly pour His Love into me, filling and saturating me with all that is good. As this love flowed in it flushed out everything not pure, not needed, and not useful. When I thought I was full I heard, "Please stretch and accept more." With Prophet's help, somehow I found more room and accepted all I could. I dropped back down to my knees and started crying with an overwhelming joy I cannot describe. Shortly afterwards Prophet returned me to my physical body back in the schoolroom.

God loves every one of His children and wants to bless and share with us His Love, peace, joy and much, much more. He wants us to know deeply that we are loved, and this gift is freely given, unearned, and by Grace, but we have to do our part and accept it. To help us, God has provided a Prophet as a guide, a Wayshower and the way. We cannot make this journey home alone. We have the opportunity to experience God's Light, Sound, and Love through and with the help of His Prophet. If accepted, this love will make your life so much sweeter, richer, and more abundant than you could possibly have ever imagined, as it has mine!

Written by Jason Levinson

48

Now I'm Sure

God provides a spiritual path perfect for each of us.
When it takes us as far as it can, we must seek a new
trail to continue our journey home to God. We should
think no less of our prior path. Instead be grateful for it
leading us to the next trailhead, especially when it
brings us to the start of our final climb.

Ever since I was a little girl I remember
struggling to find a religion that was right for me.
I was raised as an inactive Catholic until I was
about eight, and then my family joined a
Japanese religion that practiced spiritual healing.
My father was especially fond of this religion, as
it helped him out of many self-destructive habits.
The whole family was expected to feel the same
about this path.

This religion gave me a good foundation, and
I enjoyed going to church for the most part, but I
remember always feeling a sense there was
something missing and being unsettled. I recall
thinking there had to be something else out

there where I would feel at home; I knew in my heart this just was not it. In my early twenties I slowly stopped attending services as I began my search for another path. A few things I knew for sure: I loved God and Jesus and did not want to let go of that as I tried different faiths. I visited various churches but nothing quite clicked. Many acted as if their beliefs were superior, the only way, and that I should take their word for it or else I would not go to Heaven someday.

I also got involved in a bad relationship, though in hindsight I see it was a search for love. I grew so frustrated I began praying many, many times a day. I knew God had to have heard me. Many times I prayed fifteen prayers in a row, all in hopes to find peace in my life, to find God. About three months into my praying marathon the bad relationship ended, and soon after I met a special Soul who introduced me to Guidance for a Better Life. Before he took me there for the first time we spoke many times about God, religion, and such. I recall his being so respectful of my faith even though I was unsure about it myself. I was very attached to it; it was all I knew. It was strange to me at the time that someone was not trying to convert me. It definitely caught my attention. I asked him once to come to church with me and to my surprise he was genuinely happy to go. Later he shared with me that he was very happy with his faith. He mentioned he had found the place he felt the closest to God, the path that was right for him. There was zero doubt in his words and a lot of love and respect. He was so peaceful and grounded on what he was saying. Wow, I wanted what he had.

I waited anxiously for my first retreat at Guidance for a Better Life. I absolutely could not wait to go. I had seen pictures of it. It looked so beautiful nestled in the Blue Ridge Mountains. I even had a dream of meeting Del and his wife Lynne before meeting them in person. I remember during my first retreat I listened to every word Del spoke and I wanted more. It rang true. Had I found the right path for me? I wondered. It sure felt like it. As Del spoke in class his voice sounded so familiar. Soon after, I had a memory of me hearing his voice when I was a baby in my crib. How could this be? I did not understand how that was even possible, but it brought me so much comfort and peace. I could not wait to take another retreat, then another, then another. There was so much to learn!

A couple years into attending retreats, I went

to a retreat that confirmed I had found the right path for me. During it, a small number of students and I spent a week in a cabin, learning more about ourselves and strengthening our relationship with the Divine. One evening Del led us in a spiritual exercise, and we all sang HU, a pure love song to God. While singing I saw a blue ball of light with light behind it. It was alive and beautiful. Prophet then spiritually took me to the pond at the retreat center where I lay down on its dock. After that I went in the water expecting it to feel cold, but it felt nice. I saw myself getting my head dunked over and over in its water. It was beautiful and felt like I was being baptized.

I was then shown a path going uphill on a mountain. I climbed it, and was led to a spot I recognized. It was where my past spiritual teacher, the leader in the Japanese religion I used to follow, had received a revelation from God that he was to dedicate his life to serving Him. As I arrived I saw him standing there. I could not believe my eyes! I never got to meet him in person as he had passed years before I joined his religion. My heart was so happy. We spoke without words. I got a chance to express I was grateful for where he had taken me in my spiritual journey. A few seconds later I had a knowing it was time to go and I saw Prophet inviting me to go with him. Up we flew from that mountaintop to the stars in the sky. We sat together and looked back at the beautiful blue Earth. The view was magnificent. We were hundreds of miles higher up than that mountaintop.

This experience was very significant to me at that time in my life, and it still is. I had been introduced to a path that was right for me but was hesitant to leave the religion I had known. This experience told me it was okay to follow my heart. I could be grateful to the previous teachings and teachers I was blessed with and now accept these seemingly new teachings. I was reassured that my new teacher could take me much, much further if I wanted to go and was willing to do my part. What a gift experience.

My faith is now based on actual real experiences with the Divine. These experiences would not have been possible without Prophet as my teacher to guide me every step of the way. I can say with confidence I know God loves me and I love Him. I have also been taught many other truths I carry in my heart. These truths make my life more and more abundant every day.

Written by Olga Boucher

49

The Return to Heaven

God sent Souls to Earth from the heavenly worlds to grow in their ability to give and receive love, and learn about giving back to life through service to others. We have not been sent on this journey alone. The Son of God, the Prophet, has been right there with us the whole time and is ultimately the way home. The following is an incredible account from someone who experienced this round-trip journey during a contemplation.

Cool, crisp October air brushed the side of my left arm. Beyond the water of the pond, orange-gold and yellow leaves reached up into the clear blue sky like steeples crowning nature's church. The timeless beauty of the mountains nearly took my breath away. Gradually I closed my eyes. A song of HU began and grew, and I began to sing along. An amazing group of Souls, who devote their lives and hearts to God, filled the mountains with their sacred song. We sang the purest song we could, asking nothing in return.

My heart opened to the Love of God. It poured in like a waterfall. Had it been there all along?

While my outer eyes were closed, my inner vision opened wide. Somewhat like a dream, colors danced before my eyes. As we continued singing HU a form appeared in front of me. God's Prophet was before me, and he took me on a journey I would not soon forget. He took me to the golden shores of Heaven. Gentle waves were lapping on an endless sandy beach. Golden light, abundant joy, and boundless creativity filled the air with utter bliss. Splashing in the water made me feel just like a child again. What joy! What peace! What wonder here!

Suddenly and violently, everything began to shake. A mighty rumble filled the world with words I could not understand. Words like thunder — loud and low. The floor of Heaven cracked and split! Below, a dark and dismal pit. A new sensation — gravity — pulled me into the abyss, but I was not alone. Scores of Souls were screaming, tumbling deep into the lightless hole. Deeper, deeper, down and down, it seemed the fall would never end. Yet I felt another presence too, one serene, calm, and benign. The Son of God was holding me, protecting me within his arms. At first I screamed and pulled and clawed, a vain attempt to climb back up. Regardless of my struggle, I just kept falling down. So then I begged, I cried, and prayed. "Please take me home! Please take me home!" But still to no avail. The Mighty One who carried me just seemed to smile in response.

At last when all my hope was lost, I rested in the mighty arms of Prophet. I relaxed into his loving hold and felt his love surround me; the arms of strength, the arms of peace, the arms of everlasting love. I found I needed nothing else, even in this endless pit. No longer did I struggle, no longer did I beg — for everything I'd ever need was here, and now, with him. I rested in his strength and leaned into Prophet's chest. His heart opened and enveloped me. Within it was a door. A door of light. I entered it and then to my surprise, I was once again upon the sands of Heaven's ocean shore. Familiar breaking waves of gold and sand beneath my feet — and then I knew without a doubt I'd never really left.

But somehow I was different now. I was not here to splash and play, self-serving in God's Love. Having once lost this realm of bliss, on my return I loved it all the more. No longer did I feel it was a place to serve my selfish needs. Heaven is a place to give, to serve with all you have. On bended knee I lowered down onto the golden ocean shore and thanked the Lord, the God most high, for the journey I'd been on.

I'd learned a lot from my round-trip within Prophet's arms. You don't find God by searching, scrambling, trying to climb to Him. You don't find God by begging, pleading, praying to get home. You find God when you love His Prophet, love His Son, with all your heart, with all your mind, and with all you are. And when you return home to God, you may find you've never left. But don't expect to be the same as you were before the trip, for the journey will have taught you much; much more than words can say.

God *always* has a Prophet here on Earth to lead us home. The Prophet now is Del Hall III, and he lives in Virginia. He's reaching out his hand to you — will you take hold? Will you accept?

Written by David Hughes

50

Teacher of the Heart

Witnessing selfless acts of love and kindness can inspire you to do the same. This will lead you to a more abundant life. Those who have a teacher who is a living, breathing example of giving back to life in everything they do are most fortunate indeed.

At an early retreat I attended at Guidance for a Better Life there was a student who had recently lost a loved one. At the end of the retreat, Del, the teacher, handed out a small gift to each student — a blue bead that represented our personal experiences with the Divine we each had been blessed with during the retreat. He picked one out for himself, but then gave it to the student in honor of their loved one who had recently passed. I was touched deeply by this. It did not seem contrived or done for effect. It felt genuine, sincere, and from the heart.

When I arrived home that act of generosity stayed with me. It kept tugging at my heart until

I decided I had to do something, to respond to it in kind. So I sent my blue bead to Del with a short note. His small act had triggered something within me, an innate trust for him buried there. In the note I identified him as a "teacher of the heart." I am pretty sure I had never even heard that phrase before I wrote it, or given much thought to what one was. Yet I knew without a doubt that he was, and is, just such a teacher. Since that day, he has shown me I am so much happier when I give without expecting anything in return, other than the joy of giving. "Giving is its own reward," goes the old adage. It has proven to be very true in my life. It turns out I was not the only one moved by Del's simple gesture that day. Another student had in fact been similarly touched and sent their bead to Del as well.

This story is a happy one. Both I and the other student received a replacement bead at a later retreat, which I was not expecting, but was silently hoping for and overjoyed to accept. Mine will always remind me that a "Teacher of the Heart," one who teaches by lessons and by example, is a rare and precious gift. A teacher who hears and speaks to our hearts, who is fluent in the "Language of the Divine," and who is adept at reading us better than we often know ourselves. A teacher who knows how to help us be the best we can be spiritually. The kind of teacher to give us practical tools to live a better life — the abundant life God has planned for us. The kind of teacher a loving God would send to His children to help remind us He loves us and wants us to return home again.

Written by Chris Comfort

Guidance for a Better Life
Our Story

$\sim\!\!\sim\!\!\sim$

My Father's Journey

God always has a living Prophet on Earth to teach His Ways and accomplish His will. My father, Del Hall III, is currently God's true Prophet fully raised up and ordained by God Himself. He was not always a Prophet, nor did he even know what a Prophet was, but God had a plan

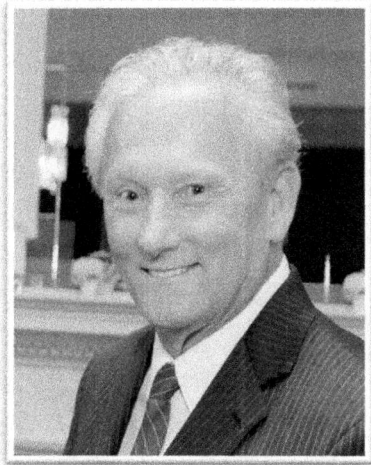

Prophet Del Hall III

for him like He has for all of His children. Over many years through many life experiences, God had begun to prepare my father for his future assignment, mostly unbeknownst to him. Everything he experienced in his life from the joys to the sadness helped prepare him for his future role as Prophet.

My dad grew up in California and was a decent student but a better athlete. He received an appointment to the United States Naval Academy in Annapolis, Maryland where he later met my mother. They were married two days after he graduated and received his commission as an officer. After a short tour on a Navy ship deployed to Vietnam, he went to flight training school and became a Navy fighter pilot. While attending flight school in Pensacola, Florida he also earned a Master of Science Degree and had the first of his three children, a son. After flight school he was stationed in a fighter squadron on the East Coast, where he and my mom began investing in real estate, adding to their family with the birth of two daughters. Following this tour of duty he was assigned as a jet flight instructor in Texas, after which, his time in the Navy was finished. He was a natural pilot and loved his time in the sky, but it was time to move on.

So far in life he had no real concern for, or even thought much about God, religion, or spiritual matters in general. He lived life fully. He raised his family. He traveled. He invested and became an entrepreneur starting and growing highly successful businesses in diverse fields ranging from real estate to aerospace consulting. Years before however, a seed had been planted when God's eternal teachings were introduced to him in his late teens, and while it did not show outwardly, the truth in these teachings spoke to his heart. My dad might not have been giving much thought about God up to this point in his life, but God was definitely thinking about him and the future He had planned for him. Like an acorn destined to become a mighty oak, the seed that lay dormant in his heart would someday be stirred to life. Through all his life experiences, both "good" and "bad," God would be preparing him for his future role as His Prophet.

When God decided it was time, He called my dad to Him. He did this by shutting down the world of financial security my dad had built. Over a period of two years all of his businesses were wound down and dissolved. What seemed like security turned out to be an illusion. Financial success had not provided true security. He now had failed businesses and a failing marriage and was trying to fix things without God's help, principles, or guidance. As painful as this time in his life was, it was yet another step towards the glorious life of service awaiting my father. God was removing him from the world my dad had created and furthering him along his path to his future role as Prophet.

After his marriage ended and his businesses wound down, he started fresh by going out west to give flying lessons near Lake Mead, Nevada. While living in Nevada my dad was reintroduced to the eternal teachings of God he first learned of as a teenager twenty-three years earlier, and though they resonated with him at the time, his priorities were different back then. Now, his serious training could begin. He started having very clear experiences with the Holy Spirit and noticed there was a familiarity with these teachings and experiences. He embraced the long hours of instruction, which often lasted until sunrise, and was receptive to the personal spiritual experiences he was given. This began an intense period of study and desire for spiritual truth that continues to this day. Some of his most profound and meaningful experiences during this time were with past Prophets of old. They came to him spiritually in contemplations and dreams. He learned of their roles in history and how they were raised up and ordained by God directly. He began to realize they were training him but was not clear why. A few times his experiences led him to believe he was in training to be a future Prophet. However, that revelation made no sense to him because he felt he was an imperfect person who made mistakes and had failures. He thought of the past and current Prophets of God as perfected Souls, not imperfect like he felt he was. Why would God choose him for such a role? He did not feel qualified.

Besides being introduced to God's teachings while he was out west, my father was blessed to meet his current wife Lynne. Returning to the East Coast, my father and Lynne moved into a small cabin on land he had acquired before his businesses shut down. This was a major change in his life, but it felt deeply right within him. He began to remember a desire to live like this as a child; from early childhood my dad found clarity and peace in nature. He had forgotten about this until now, but God had not and made this dream a reality. In addition to being their home, these beautiful, three-hundred-plus acres of land in the Blue Ridge Mountains would eventually become the location for the Guidance for a Better Life retreat center. The perfection of my father's experiences from earlier in his life in real estate, providing the land for his next step in life, speaks to the perfection of God's plan. One of many many examples I could list.

For many years my dad took wilderness skills courses around the country. He specialized in the study of wild edible and medicinal plants, tracking, and awareness skills, and authored articles for publication. Inspired to help folks feel more comfortable in the outdoors, my dad and Lynne began the Nature Awareness School in 1990. Classes were focused on teaching awareness and the primitive living skills needed to enjoy the woods and survive in them if necessary. An amazing thing happened within those first few years though; students began to experience aspects of God in very personal and dramatic ways. Somewhat like my dad's experience out west, they found that stepping away from their daily routine and the hustle of life, if even for a few days, created space for Spirit to do Its work. Whether they were enjoying the beauty of the Virginia wilderness and tranquility of the school grounds or relaxing by the pond, he found students' hearts opened, and they became more receptive to the Divine Hand that is always reaching out to Its children.

More and more the discourse during wilderness classes shifted to the meanings of dreams, personal growth, finding balance in life, and experiences the students were having with the Voice of God in Its many forms. An increase of spiritual retreats was offered to fulfill the demand and over time became the predominant class offerings; the wilderness survival skills classes eventually fading away completely. The name "Nature Awareness School" seemed to be less fitting for what was actually being taught now and in February 2019 my father changed the name of the retreat center to Guidance for a Better Life.

Throughout this time my father's training and spiritual study continued. My father reached mastership and was ordained by God on July 7, 1999 but he was still not yet Prophet, more was required. On October 22, 2012, twenty-five years since his full-time intensive training had begun, God ordained him as His chosen Prophet, and He has continued to raise him up further since. God works through my father in very direct and beneficial ways for his students. Hundreds and hundreds of students for more than thirty years have received God's eternal teachings through my father's instruction and mentoring. They have had personal experiences with the Divine which have transformed and greatly blessed their lives. My father's greatest joy is being used by God as a servant to share God's ways and truths with thirsty Souls and hungry seekers. In addition to mountaintop retreats, my father continues to spread God's ways and teachings that so greatly blessed his life and the lives of his loved ones in many ways, including his books and videos.

Maybe you are at a turning point in your life and looking for direction. Maybe you have a knowing there is more to life but not sure what that might be or how to find it. Or, maybe you are simply drawn to what you read and hear in our stories. God speaks to our hearts and calls each of us in many different ways. Like my father's journey demonstrates, it doesn't matter where you started or the twists, turns, or seeming dead-ends your life has taken; God wants us to know Him more fully, and for us to know our purpose within His creation. He wants us to experience His Love regardless of our religious path or lack thereof. He always has a living Prophet here on Earth to help us accomplish His desire for us — to show us the way home to Him and to experience more abundance in our lives while we are still living here on Earth. God's Prophet today is my father, Del Hall III. You have the opportunity to grow spiritually through God's teachings which Prophet shares. His guidance for a better life is available for you — please accept it.

Written by Del Hall IV

My Son, Del Hall IV

My son, Del Hall IV, joined Guidance for a Better Life as an instructor after fifteen years of in-class training with me, his father. He helped develop the five-step Keys to Spiritual Freedom Study Program and facilitates the first two courses in the

Del Hall IV

program: Step One "Tools to Recognize Divine Guidance" and Step Two "Understanding Divine Guidance." Del also teaches people about the rich history of dream study and how to better recall their own dreams during the Dream Study Workshops, which he hosts around the country. He is qualified to step in and facilitate any of my retreats should the need arise.

Del authored the book *God is in the Garden*, a priceless book of wisdom in the form of parables. Through stories of everyday events of life on the mountain Del shares profound insights into the nature of God and life that are infused with his natural humor and unique perspective.

Del is also Vice President of Marketing and helps with everything required to get the "good news" from Guidance for a Better Life out to hungry seekers: everything from book publishing, blogging, and posting on social media outlets. He is co-author and book cover designer for many of our, thus far, twenty published books.

My son loves the opportunity to work on creative projects for Guidance for a Better Life. From a very early age he has been an artist and loved creating artwork in multiple mediums. He was accepted into gifted art programs in Virginia Beach, Virginia and then after high school graduation he attended the School of the Museum of Fine Arts in Boston. He is now a nationally exhibited artist and his *Paintings of the Light and Sound of God* are in over two hundred public and private collections. One of the greatest joys of the painting process for Del is using his paintings as an opportunity to share with others the inspiration behind them, God's

Love and his experiences with the Light and Sound of God, the Holy Spirit, in contemplation and in waking life.

Del lives on the retreat center property in the Blue Ridge Mountains of Virginia with his wife where they raised and homeschooled my three grandchildren. Recently he helped me with an extensive renovation and update for the three hand-built log cabins on retreat center property originally used for advanced spiritual retreats. He loves woodworking, tending to his vegetable garden, pruning his fruit trees, and helping maintain the beautiful three-hundred acres of retreat center property for students to enjoy. There is always something that needs attention on the land and Del is always up to the challenge. He loves to travel and spends his free time enjoying this beautiful country with his family in their RV.

My son has had multiple brain surgeries starting when he was seventeen years old for a recurring brain tumor. He credits God for surviving and thriving all this time when most with his condition do not. He looks to the sunrise every day with gratitude for yet another chance at life. With that chance he desires to help me share the love and teachings of God that have so blessed our lives. I pray to God daily thanking Him for my son's good health.

Written by Prophet Del Hall

What is the Role of God's Prophet?

An introductory understanding of God's handpicked and Divinely trained Prophet is necessary to fully benefit from reading this book. God ALWAYS has a living Prophet of His choice on Earth. He has a physical body with a limited number of students, but the inner spiritual side of Prophet is limitless. Spiritually he can help countless numbers of Souls all over the world, no matter what religion or path they are on — even if that is no path at all. He teaches the ways of God and shares the Light and Sound of God. He delivers the living Word of God. Prophet can teach you physically as well as through dreams, and he can lift you into the Heavens of God. He offers protection, peace, teachings, guidance, healing, and love.

Each of God's Prophets throughout history has a unique mission. One may only have a few students with the sole intent to keep God's teachings and truth alive. God may use another to change the course of history. God's Prophets are usually trained by both the current and former Prophets. The Prophet is tested and trained over a very long period of time. The earlier Prophets are physically gone but teach the new Prophet in the inner spiritual worlds. This serves two main purposes: the trainee becomes very adept at spiritual travel and gains wisdom from those in whose shoes he will someday walk. This is vital training because the Prophet is the one who must safely prepare and then take his students into the Heavens and back.

There are many levels of Heaven, also called planes or mansions. Saint Paul once claimed to know a man who went to the third Heaven. Actually it was Paul himself that went, but the pearl is, if there is a third Heaven, it presumes a first and second Heaven also exist. The first Heaven is often referred to as the Astral plane. Even on just that one plane of existence there are over one hundred sub-planes. This Heaven is where most people go after passing, unless they receive training while still here in their physical body. Without a guide who is trained properly in the ways of God a student could misunderstand the intended lesson and become confused as to what is truth. The inner worlds are enormous compared to the physical worlds. They are very real and can be explored safely when guided by God's Prophet.

Part of my mission is to share more of what is spiritually possible for you as a child of God. Few Souls know or understand that God's Prophet can safely guide God's children, while still alive physically, to their Heavenly Home. Taking a child of God into the Heavens is not the job of clergy. Clergy have a responsibility to pass on the teaching of their religion exactly as they were taught, not to add additional concepts or possibilities. If every clergy member taught their own personal belief system no religion could survive for long. Then the beautiful teachings of an earlier Prophet of God would be lost. Clergy can be creative in finding interesting and uplifting ways to share their teachings, but their job is to keep their religion intact. However, God sends His Prophets to build on the teachings of His past Prophets, to share God's Light and Love, to teach His language, and to guide Souls to their Heavenly Home.

There is ALWAYS MORE when it comes to God's teachings and truth. No one Prophet can teach ALL of God's ways. It may be that the audience of a particular time in history cannot absorb more wisdom. It could be due to a

Prophet's limited time to teach and limited time in a physical body on Earth. Ultimately, it is that there is ALWAYS MORE! Each of God's Prophets brings additional teachings and opportunities for ways to draw closer to God, building on the work and teachings of former Prophets. That is one reason why Prophets of the past ask God to send another; to comfort, teach, and continue to help God's children grow into greater abundance. Former Prophets continue to have great love for God's children and want to see them continue to grow in accepting more of God's Love. One never needs to stop loving or accepting help from a past Prophet in order to grow with the help of the current Prophet. All true Prophets of God work together and help one another to do God's work.

All the testimonies in this book were written by students at the Guidance for a Better Life retreat center. It is here that the nature of God, the Holy Spirit, and the nature of Soul are EXPERIENCED under the guidance of a true living Prophet of God. Guidance for a Better Life is NOT a religion, it is a retreat center. God and His Prophet are NOT disparaging of any religion of love. However, the more a path defines itself with its teachings, dogma, or tenets, the more "walls" it inadvertently creates between the seeker and God. Sometimes it even puts God into a smaller box. God does not fit in any box. Prophet is for all Souls and is purposely not officially aligned with any path, but shows respect to all.

YOU can truly have an ABUNDANT LIFE through a personal and loving relationship with God, the Holy Spirit, and God's ordained Prophet. This is my primary message to you. Having a closer relationship with the Divine requires understanding the "Language of the Divine." God expresses His Love to us, His children, in many different and sometimes very subtle ways. Often His Love goes unrecognized and unaccepted because His language is not well known. The testimonies in this book have shown you some of the ways in which God expresses His Love. It is my hope that in reading this book, you have begun to learn more of the "Language of the Divine." The stories spanned from very subtle Divine guidance to profound examples of experiencing God up close and very personal. After reading this book I hope you now know your relationship with God has the potential to be more profound, more personal, and more loving than any organized religion on Earth currently teaches.

If you wish to develop a relationship with God's Prophet, seek the inner side of Prophet, for he is spiritually already with you. Few are able to meet the current physical incarnation and most people do not need to meet Prophet physically. Gently sing HU for a few minutes and then sing "Prophet" with love in your heart and he will respond. It may take time to recognize his presence, but it will come. The Light and Love that flows through him is the same that has flowed through all of God's true Prophets.

A more abundant life awaits you,

Prophet Del Hall III

Articles of Faith

Written by Prophet Del Hall III

1. There is one true God who is still living and active in our lives. He is knowable and wants a relationship with each of His children. He is the same God Jesus called FATHER and is known by many names, including Heavenly Father, and the ancient names for God, HU, and Sugmad (Pronounced SOOG-mahd). God wants a loving, trusting, personal relationship with each of us, NOT one based upon fear or guilt.

2. The Holy Spirit is God's expression in all the worlds. It is in two parts, the Light and the Sound. It is through His Holy Spirit God communicates and delivers all His gifts: peace, clarity, love, joy, healings, correction, guidance, wisdom, comfort, truth, dreams, new revelations, and more.

3. God always has a chosen living Prophet to teach His ways, speak His Living Word, lift up Souls, and bring us closer to God. God's living Prophet is a concentrated aspect of the Holy Spirit, the Light and Sound, and is raised up and ordained by God directly. His Prophet is

empowered and authorized to share God's Light and Sound and to correct misunderstandings of His ways. There are two aspects of God's Prophet, an inner spiritual and outer physical Prophet. The inner Prophet can teach us through dreams, intuition, spiritual travel, inner communication, and his presence. The outer Prophet also teaches through his discourses, written word, and his presence. There is no separation between the inner and outer Prophet. Both inner and outer aspects of Prophet are concentrated aspects of the Holy Spirit. Prophet is always with us spiritually on the inner. Prophet points to and glorifies the Father.

4. God so loves the world and His children He has always had a long unbroken line of His chosen Prophets on Earth. They existed before Jesus and after Jesus. Jesus was God's Prophet and His actual SON. God's chosen Prophets are considered to be in the "role of God's son," though NOT literally His Son. Only Jesus was literally His Son. Prophets were sometimes called Paraclete. The Bible uses the word Comforter, but the original Greek word was Paraclete, which is more accurate. Paraclete implies an actual physical person who helps, counsels,

encourages, advocates, comforts, sets free, and more.

5. Our real and eternal self is called Soul. We are Soul; we do NOT "have" a Soul. As Soul we are literally an individualized piece of God's Holy Spirit, thereby divine in nature. As an individual and uniquely experienced Soul you have free will, intelligence, imagination, opinions, clear and continuous access to Divine guidance, and immortality. As Soul we have an innate and profound spiritual growth potential. Soul has the ability to travel the Heavens spiritually with Prophet to gain truth and wisdom and grow in love. Soul exists because God loves It.

6. We have one eternal life as Soul. However, Soul needs to incarnate many times into a physical body to learn and grow spiritually mature. Soul's long journey back home to God where It was first created encompasses many lifetimes. A loving God does not expect His children to learn His ways in a single lifetime.

7. Soul equals Soul, in that God loves all Souls equally and each Soul has the same innate qualities and potential. Soul is neither male nor female, any particular race, nationality, or age. When Soul comes into a physical body at birth, the physical body is male or female, a certain

race, a nationality, and has an age. All Souls are children of God. We do not have to earn God's Love; He loves us unconditionally.

8. Soul incarnates on Earth to grow in the ability to give and receive love and learn to live the way God wishes us to live. Because God loves us, His ways of living create abundant, happy, fulfilling lives. His beautiful ways of living are mostly HOW to live, and less on what NOT to do.

9. God is more interested in two Souls learning to love one another regardless of their sexual preference. God loves you just the way you are.

10. It is God's will that a negative power exists to help Soul grow spiritually through challenges and hardships, thereby strengthening and maturing Soul. We are never given a challenge greater than our ability to find a solution to or understand the necessary lesson, if we use our God-given creativity, make sufficient personal effort, and ask for and accept the help available from the Divine. Soul has the ability to rise above any obstacles with God's help.

11. We study the Bible as an authentic teaching tool of God's ways, in addition to books and discourses authored by a Prophet chosen by God. We know the original biblical writings are

sometimes misunderstood, for example, God loves each of us regardless of our errors and shortcomings. God's eternal abandonment or damnation is not true. He would never turn His back to us for eternity. (Isaiah 54:7-8 and 10, Lamentations 3:31-32, and Hebrews 13:5)

12. Karma is the way in which the Divine accounts for our actions, words, thoughts, and attitudes. One can create positive or negative karma. Karma is a blessing used to teach us responsibility.

13. A child is not born in sin, however, the child does have karma from former lives. Karma, God's accounting system, explains our birth circumstances better than the concept of sin.

14. A living Prophet, including Jesus, can remove karma and sin when necessary to help us get started or to grow on the path home to God. However, it is primarily our responsibility to live and grow in the ways of God, thereby not creating negative karma and sin.

15. There are four commandments of God in which we abide: First — Love God with all your heart, mind, and Soul; Second — Love your neighbor as yourself. The Third is, "Seek ye first the Kingdom of God, and His righteousness."

This means that it is primarily our responsibility to draw close to God, learn His ways, and strive to live the way God would like us to live. God's Prophet is sent to show His ways. Our purpose, the Fourth Commandment, is to become spiritually mature to be used by God to bless His children. Becoming a coworker with God through His Comforter is our primary purpose in life and the most rewarding attainment of Soul.

16. All Souls upon translation, death of the physical body, go to the higher worlds, called Heavens, planes, or mansions, regardless of their beliefs. The way they live life on Earth and the effort made to draw close to God impacts the area of Heaven they are to be sent. Those who purposely harm others (except in defense of self or others), themselves, or live against the ways of God go to unpleasant locations on the first Heaven; to a location where they can learn how to do better, as a gift of love. The first Heaven has a wide range of locations, from very very unpleasant and hellish, to wonderful and beautiful places to spend time with loved ones while learning and preparing for future incarnations. Those who draw close to a Prophet of God, including Jesus, receive special care. We know of twelve distinct Heavens, not one. The

primary Abode of the Heavenly Father is in the twelfth Heaven, known as the Ocean of Love and Mercy. We can visit God while we still live on Earth, if taken by His chosen Prophet and only as Soul, not in a physical body.

17. Prayer is sacred, personal exchange with God and is an extreme privilege. God hears every prayer from the heart whether or not we recognize a response. Singing an ancient name of God, HU, is our foundational prayer. It expresses love and gratitude to God and is unencumbered by words. Singing HU has the potential to raise us up in consciousness making us more receptive to God's Love, Light, and guiding Hand. After praying it is best to spend time listening to God. Prayer should never be rote or routine. We desire to trust God and to know His will for us, and then freely and joyfully surrender to His will rather than our own will. God's Prophet can teach us the "Language of the Divine" which will help us understand how God communicates with us and help us recognize God's Love in our lives.

18. It is our responsibility to stay spiritually nourished. When Soul is nourished and fortified It becomes activated, and we are more receptive and have clearer communication with the Divine.

When Jesus said, "Give us this day our daily bread," he meant daily spiritual nourishment, not physical bread. The Holy Spirit is nourishment for Soul. This can be received by singing HU, studying Scripture, praying, dream study, demonstrating gratitude for our blessings, being in a living Prophet's physical presence or in his inner presence, or listening to his words.

19. TRUTH has the power to improve every area of our lives, but only if understood, accepted, and integrated into our lives.

20. God and His Prophet guide us in our sleeping dreams and awake dreams as a gift of love. God's Prophet teaches how to understand both types of dreams. All areas of our lives may be blessed by the wisdom God offers each of us directly in dreams.

21. Gratitude is extremely important on the path of love. It is literally the secret of love. Developing an attitude of gratitude is necessary to becoming spiritually mature. Recognizing and being grateful for the blessings of God in our lives is vital to building a loving and trusting relationship with God and His chosen Prophet. A relationship with God's Prophet is THE KEY to everything good. This includes a more abundant

life filled with the Treasures of Heaven Jesus taught about in Matthew 6.

22. We are to be good stewards of our blessings. We recognize them as gifts of love from God and make the effort to have remembrance. Remembering our blessings helps to keep our hearts open to God and builds trust in God's Love for us.

23. We give others the respect and freedom to have their own beliefs, make their own choices, and live their lives as they wish. We expect the same in return.

24. The Love and blessings of God and His Prophet are available to all who are receptive. If one desires guidance and help from Prophet, ask from the heart and sing "Prophet." He will respond. One does not need to meet Prophet physically to receive help because he is a concentrated aspect of God's Holy Spirit, and is always with us. To be taught by Prophet in the physical is a sacred blessing. Much can be gained by reading or listening to the Heavenly Father's teachings being shared by Prophet.

25. We have a responsibility to do our part and let God and His Prophet do their part. This responsibility brings freedom. Our goal is to

remain spiritually nourished, live the ways of God, live in balance with a core peace, and serve God as a coworker through His Comforter. We pray to use our God-given free will in a way that our actions, thoughts, words, and attitudes testify and bear witness to the Glory and Love of God.

26. There is always more to learn and grow in God's ways and truth. One cannot remain the same spiritually. One must make the effort to move forward or risk falling backward. To grow in consciousness and love requires change. Spiritual wisdom gained during our earthly incarnations can be taken to the other worlds when we translate, and into future lifetimes, unlike our physical possessions that remain in the physical.

Contact Information

Guidance for a Better Life is a worldwide mentoring program provided by Prophet Del Hall III and his son Del Hall IV. Personal one-on-one mentoring at our retreat center is our premier offering and the most direct and effective way to grow spiritually. Spiritual tools, guided exercises, and in-depth discourses on the eternal teachings of God are provided to help one become more aware of and receptive to His Holy Spirit and the abundance that awaits. With this personally-tailored guidance one begins to more fully recognize God's Love daily in their lives, both the dramatic and the very subtle. Over time our mentoring reduces fear, worry, anxiety, lack of purpose, feelings of unworthiness, guilt, and confusion; replacing those negative aspects of life with an abundance of peace, clarity, joy, wisdom, love, and self-respect leading to a more personal relationship with God, more than most know is possible. We also offer our videos, and more than twenty inspirational and educational books.

Guidance for a Better Life
P.O. Box 219
Lyndhurst, Virginia 22952
(540) 377-6068
contact@guidanceforabetterlife.com
www.guidanceforabetterlife.com

"A Growing Testament to the Power of God's Love One Profound Book at a Time."

If you could only read one of Prophet Del Hall's books this is the one. It is full of Keys to unlock the treasures of Heaven and bring more of God's Love into your life.

Spiritual Keys
For a More Abundant Life
PROPHET DEL HALL

Wayshowers are God's special emissaries to Earth. Our Heavenly Father loves us so much He has never left us alone without a Wayshower to teach us His true ways. This book explores the amazing history of God's chosen and ordained Wayshowers from thirty-five thousand years ago to today through specific examples of both well-known and little-known Wayshowers.

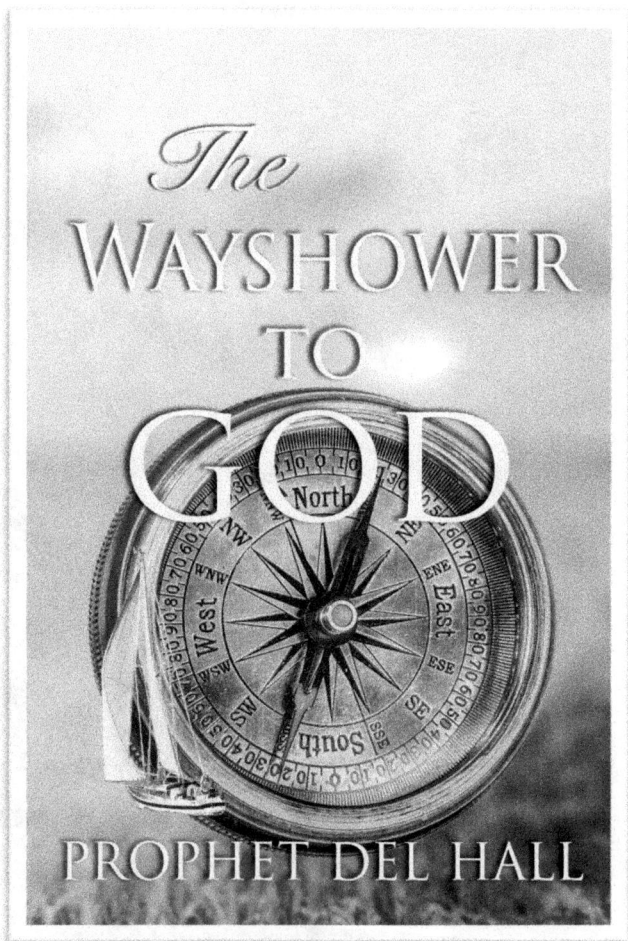

The WAYSHOWER TO GOD

PROPHET DEL HALL

GOD IS IN THE GARDEN
PARABLES

Regardless of what your venture is in life you can benefit from this unassuming book. It may appear small, but the parables contained within have the power to affect your life in extraordinary ways.

GOD
IS IN THE
Garden

PARABLES
BY DEL HALL IV

ZOOM WITH PROPHET

Guidance for a Better Life retreat center has been hosting in-person mountaintop retreats at our beautiful location in the Blue Ridge Mountains of Virginia since 1990. When the pandemic began in 2020, it inspired us to get creative with how to connect with our students and new seekers. It was then our *Zoom With Prophet* meeting series was born. Some of these Zoom meetings are now being put into book form for those who could not attend.

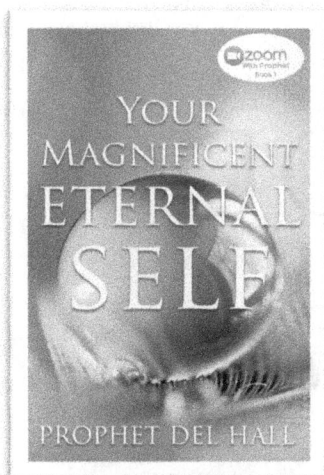

YOUR MAGNIFICENT ETERNAL SELF — PROPHET DEL HALL

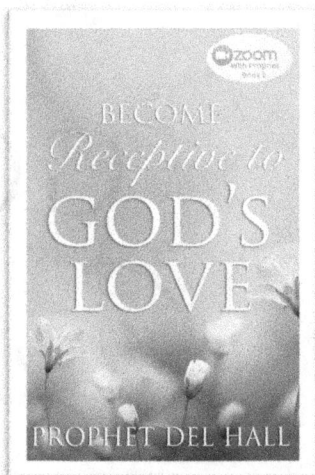

BECOME Receptive to GOD'S LOVE — PROPHET DEL HALL

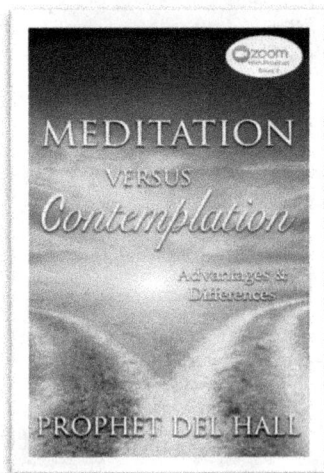

MEDITATION VERSUS Contemplation — Advantages & Differences — PROPHET DEL HALL

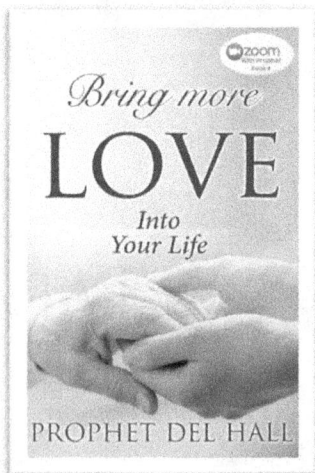

Bring more LOVE Into Your Life — PROPHET DEL HALL

SPECIALIZED TOPICS

Whether you wish to reconnect with a loved one who has passed, understand how you too can experience God's Light, improve your marriage, or learn how to understand your dreams, these incredible books have you covered.

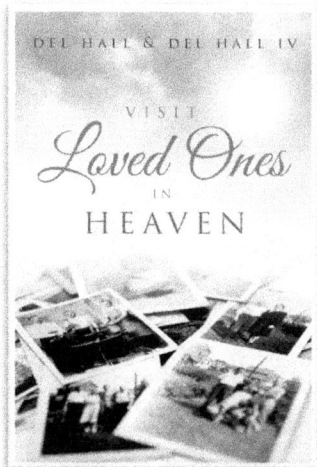

DEL HALL & DEL HALL IV

VISIT

Loved Ones

IN

HEAVEN

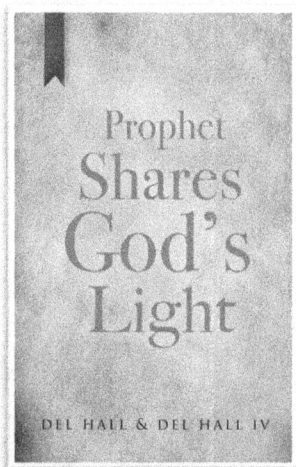

Prophet
Shares
God's
Light

DEL HALL & DEL HALL IV

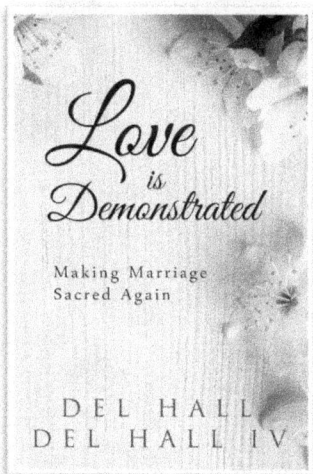

Love
is
Demonstrated

Making Marriage
Sacred Again

DEL HALL
DEL HALL IV

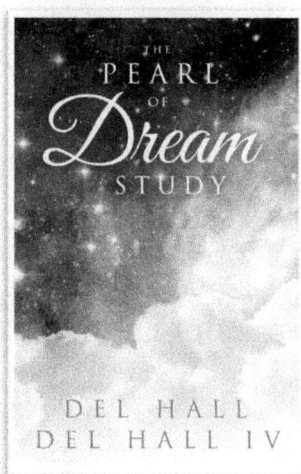

THE
PEARL
OF
Dream
STUDY

DEL HALL
DEL HALL IV

TESTIMONIES OF GOD'S LOVE SERIES

God expresses His Love every day in many different and sometimes subtle ways. Often this love goes unrecognized because the ways in which God communicates are not well known. Each of the books in this series contains fifty true stories that will help you learn to better recognize the Love of God in your life.

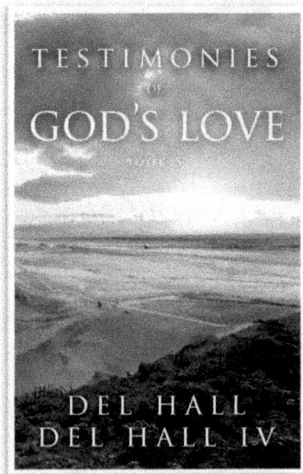

JOURNEY TO A TRUE SELF-IMAGE SERIES

This series includes intimate and unique stories that many readers will be able to personally identify with, enjoy, and learn from. They will help the reader transcend the false images people often carry about themselves — first and foremost that they are only their physical mind and body. The authors share their journeys of recognizing and coming to more fully accept their true self-image, that of Soul — an eternal child of God.

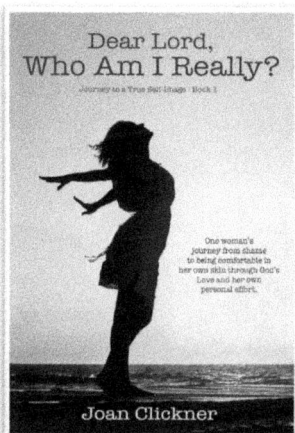

Dear Lord, Who Am I Really?
Journey to a True Self-Image · Book 1
One woman's journey from shame to being comfortable in her own skin through God's Love and her own personal effort.
Joan Clickner

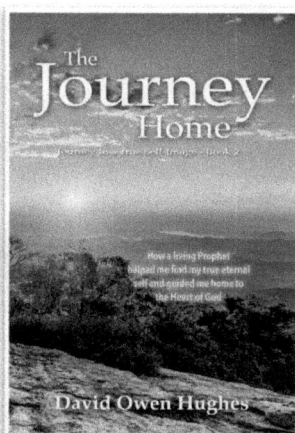

The Journey Home
Journey to a True Self-Image · Book 2
How a living Prophet helped me find my true eternal self and guided me home to the Heart of God.
David Owen Hughes

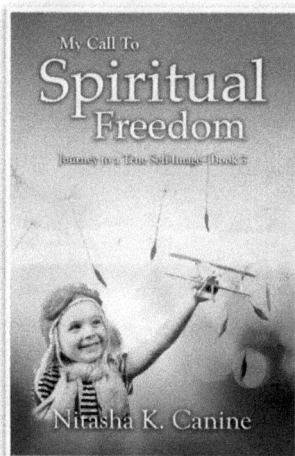

My Call To Spiritual Freedom
Journey to a True Self-Image · Book 3
Nitasha K. Canine

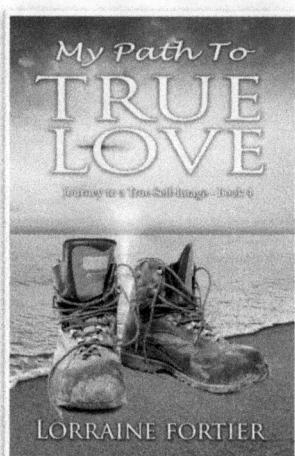

My Path To TRUE LOVE
Journey to a True Self-Image · Book 4
LORRAINE FORTIER